The Korean Go Association's

Learn to Play Go

Volume I: A Master's Guide to the Ultimate Game

Janice Kim **3 dan**

Jeong Soo-hyun **9 dan**

Drawings by a lee

Good Move Press

Published by
Good Move Press / Samarkand
www.samarkand.net

2nd printing March 1999
3rd printing March 2000
4th printing April 2002
5th printing January 2003
6th printing April 2004
7th printing May 2006
8th printing May 2008
9th printing October 2009
10th printing June 2010

ISBN 1453632891
EAN-13 9781453632895

CONTENTS

Part II: Basic Techniques

INTRODUCTION

Imagine that God has a house. It's rather large, and one of its remarkable aspects is that it contains the best examples of anything you can think of — the best chairs and tables, artworks, books, smells, all in perfectly proportioned rooms of an ideal size. If you were visiting for the evening, you might walk through the front doors and leave your coat in the hall closet to your left. The closet has a top shelf, and if you looked closely, in the far corner tucked away you might find a Go set.

The game of Go appears to have magical characteristics. The kids who usually run a circle around the prized vase sit in silent thought. The parents want the kids to stay up past bedtime for "one last game." Ancient enemies laugh together. The bank executive and the doorman make arrangements to meet for lunch. People fall in love.

Go appeals to all kinds of people, but they seem to share a characteristic: they don't like being told what to do, they don't like being told some dog-shaped cloud is really a bear. No one can say really what Go is, how you should play it, what it ought to mean to you. That can only be a personal discovery, perhaps with the aid of a native guide pointing out the features of the terrain. Learn to play Go. It is simple, but it is not easy. It is worth the time you spend on it. This is to be expected of the best kind of game.

PART 1

FUNDAMENTALS

The basic rules of Go are easy. You can become a Go player in one afternoon.

In Part I, you will see what kind of game Go is, and how it is played.

① WHAT IS GO

Go is a game that two people play with a Go board and Go stones. The players take turns putting black and white stones on the board to surround area, or **territory**. *Whoever has more territory at the end of the game is the winner.*

1.   THE BOARD AND STONES

Diagram 1:

This is a picture of a Go board. It has intersections formed by evenly spaced lines.

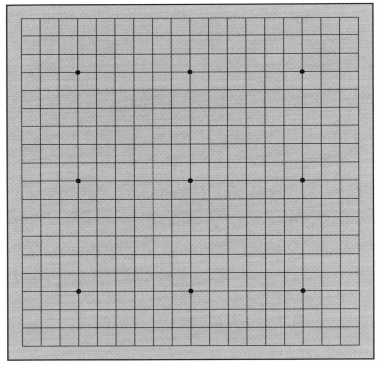

Diagram 1

There are nineteen horizontal and nineteen vertical lines on the standard board. There are 361 intersections called **points** formed by the 19 x 19 grid. There are nine darker points called **star points**, used to locate your position.

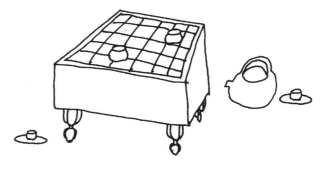

The most common standard board is about 16½ by 17¾ inches (42 cm by 45 cm), and is made of light-colored, light-grained wood. Traditionally the lines are drawn with a special black ink and are very slightly raised, but most modern boards have black lines printed or screened on wood or a wood-like playing surface. Boards vary from table versions ¼ to 2½ inches thick, to traditional floor boards with carved wooden legs.

Diagram 2:

Here are the names of the areas on the board. The corners, sides, and center are not exact, but refer to the area around a star point. Upper, lower, left, and right are from where the player with the black stones is sitting. If you are holding this book right side up, you are looking at this board from Black's point of view.

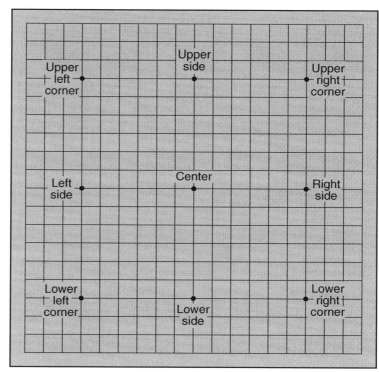

Diagram 2

Diagram 3:

Instead of a standard 19 x 19 grid, a smaller one may be used, especially when learning Go for the first time. This is a 13 x 13 grid. The most common sizes for a Go grid are 19 x 19, 13 x 13, and 9 x 9, but you could play Go on a grid of any size, even a larger or differently-shaped one. An average game on a 19 x 19 grid might take an hour, or fifteen minutes on a 9 x 9.

Nowadays Go stones usually are made of a kind of ceramic glass. Traditionally clam shell was used for the white stones, and slate for the black, but this is now expensive. Stones are kept in Go bowls with loose-fitting lids, traditionally made of

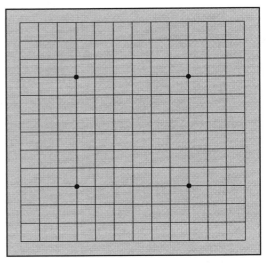

Diagram 3

wood. A standard set of stones has 181 black stones are 180 white stones (one for each point on the board) but it's no problem if you have a few less, you don't need them all to play since many points on the board will be open at the end of a game.

Go stones are held like this...   **not like this.**

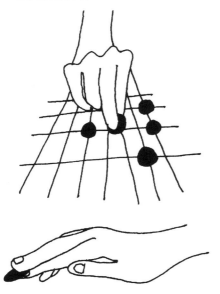

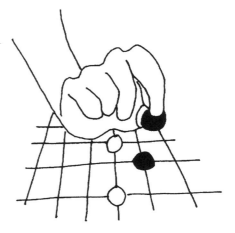

2. HOW THE GAME IS PLAYED

1. Two people sit face to face with the board between them.

Notice on most boards, one side is slightly longer than the other. The players should sit on the shorter ends. Traditionally, the older person sits at the front. How do you determine the front of a symmetrical board, you ask? In the old days, the front was the point furthest from the door of the room, as strategically, this is the point of greatest safety from attackers. Nowadays this is more a gesture of politeness.

2. The stronger player takes the white stones.

If the two players' abilities are similar, they "choose for color." First, the older player takes a handful of white stones, and the younger player guesses odd or even. You can put one or two black stones down instead of saying "odd" or "even" and take the black stones if you guess correctly. Black has an advantage.

3. The player with the black stones begins.

Take one stone between your index and middle fingers and place it on a point on the board. You can put your stone on any point you like; for the first move on a 19 x 19 grid you can choose any one of the 361 unoccupied intersections (in practice however we usually play our first move in the upper right corner around the star point).

Diagrams 4 & 5:

Don't put the stones on the lines or in the squares. Put them exactly on the points. The squares are meaningless.

<table>
<tr><td align="center">***Like this...***</td><td align="center">***not like this.***</td></tr>
<tr><td>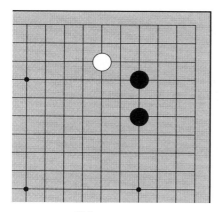</td><td>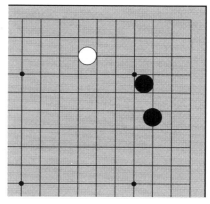</td></tr>
<tr><td align="center">*Diagram 4*</td><td align="center">*Diagram 5*</td></tr>
</table>

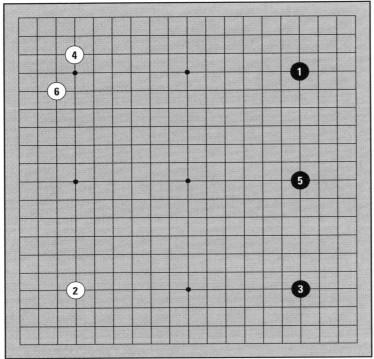

Diagram 6

Diagram 6:

The players are referred to as "Black" and "White." The number on each stone is the order in which it is played. To review this diagram, find the point on your board where Black 1 was played and put the first stone there, then put White 2, and so on. Each stone is played one at a time. You can't play two stones at once.

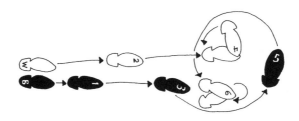

In an **even game** (one between opponents of more or less equal ability) players start with an empty board and Black makes the first move. If there is a gap between the players' abilities, the weaker player needs a head start to make the game more balanced. A **handicap game** begins with some black stones already on the board, and White makes the first move.

Diagram 7:

Here Black has four handicap stones, one in each corner, and White played the first move. Play continues as in an even game.

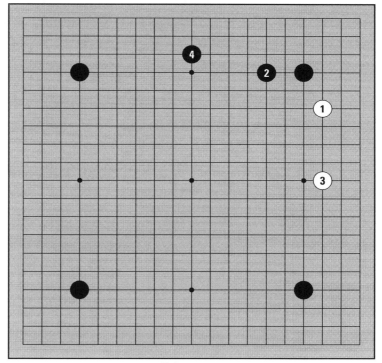

Diagram 7

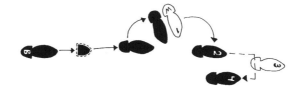

4. **At the end of the game, compare the size of Black's and White's territory. Whoever has more territory wins.**

Diagram 8:

Territory consists of the points surrounded by stones of the same color. The points surrounded by the black stones are Black territory and the points surrounded by the white stones are White territory. In this diagram, whose territory is larger? If you count the number of points, you can determine the size of the territory.

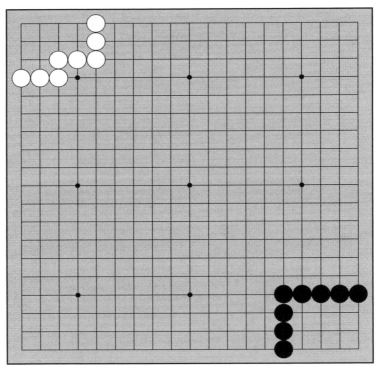

Diagram 8

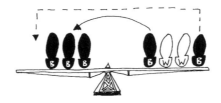

Diagram 9:

Each point of territory is marked with an ◆. By counting the number of ◆s, we see that Black has twelve points and White has ten points, so Black has two points more. If this game were over, Black would win by two points. However, there may be still more territory made in other areas on the board. At the end of the game, you have to compare the size of all the territories to determine the winner. The player with more territory overall wins.

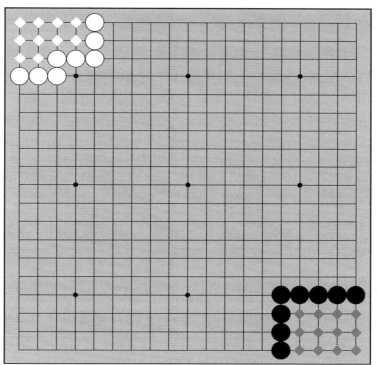

Diagram 9

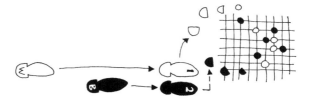

TRY IT YOURSELF

Problem 1:

There are _____ star points on the standard board.

Problem 2:

The standard board has _____ by _____ lines.

Problem 3:

The stronger player takes the _____ stones.

Problem 4:

Stones are played on the _____.

Problem 5:

_____ plays first in an even game.

Problem 6:

Whoever has the most _____ is the winner.

Problem 7:

How many points does Black have?

Problem 8:

How many points are there in White's territory?

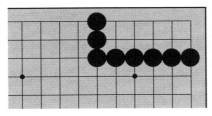

Problem 7

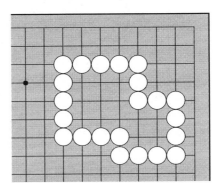

Problem 8

TRY IT YOURSELF

Problem 9:

Who has more territory?

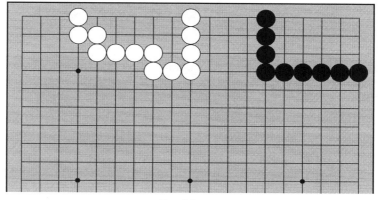

Problem 9

Problem 10:

If this is the end of the game, who wins?

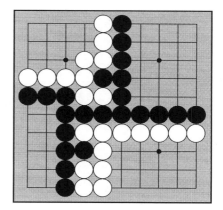

Problem 10

ANSWERS

1. 9

2. 19, 19

3. white

4. points

5. Black

6. territory

7. 10 points

8. 13 points

9. Black (5 points more)

10. Black (by 4 points)

② CAPTURING

In the battle for territory, you may capture your opponent's stones, or your stones may be captured.

1. LIBERTIES

Diagram 1:

One black stone is on the board. Notice the lines coming out from it. These lines are the stone's **liberties**. This is a translation of Chinese characters which mean "the way of activity" or "the road of life."

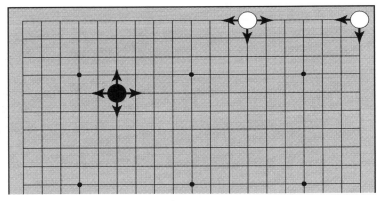

Diagram 1

A stone in the middle has four liberties. A stone on the edge has three liberties. A stone in the extreme corner has only two liberties.

2.   CAPTURE

What happens when all the liberties of a stone are blocked?

Diagram 2:

Four black stones are blocking all the liberties of the white stone. There are no lines coming out from it, so White is surrounded completely. Stones without any liberties are **captured**. Once stones are captured, they are taken off the board.

Diagram 3:

This is the result of capturing the white stone. Stones that you have captured are like prisoners of war. These stones are put in the lid of your bowl. Keep track of your prisoners, as they have value.

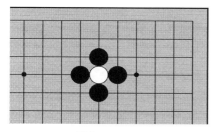

Diagram 2

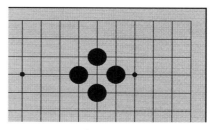

Diagram 3

Diagram 4:

On the edges, three of your stones are needed to capture your opponent's stone. In the extreme corners, just two stones are needed.

Stones without liberties are like soldiers that have been surrounded completely. They are removed from the board and held prisoner in the lids of the bowls. **Except when captured, stones do not move.**

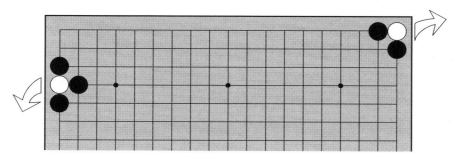

Diagram 4

3. ATARI

Stones with only one liberty are said to be in **atari**. Stones in atari can be captured on the next move. It is not necessary to say atari when you play a move that threatens to capture your opponent's stone. In Japanese, atari means a "hit." It is called *dansoo* in Korean, meaning "single" or "only one."

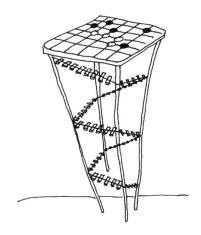

Diagram 5:

Three of the white stone's liberties are blocked. It has only one liberty left, so it is in atari. If Black puts another stone at A, the white stone is captured.

If it is White's turn, she can **run** by playing at A. Actually, you can't move a stone, but you can play another stone, linking the stone in danger to a stone on safer ground.

Diagram 6:

If White plays at 1, the original stone has not moved, but it is no longer in atari. Black cannot capture it with his next move.

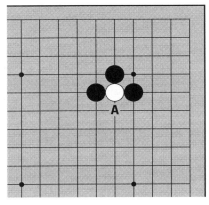

Diagram 5

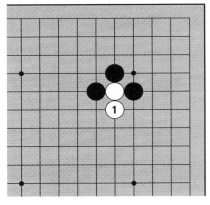

Diagram 6

4. Capturing More than One Stone

No matter how many stones there are, if all their liberties are blocked, the stones are captured.

Diagram 7:

Here are two white stones. How can Black capture them?

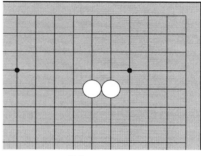

Diagram 7

Diagram 8:

Black can block all White's liberties in six moves. (Black and White take turns, so White must have chosen to play five moves elsewhere.)

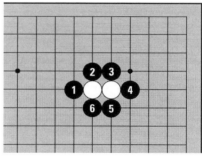

Diagram 8

Diagram 9:

This is the result of capturing the two white stones. Black has two prisoners and two points of territory.

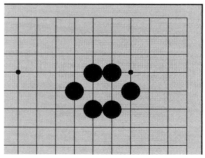

Diagram 9

Diagram 10:

Three or more stones that have no liberties are also captured. If you capture stones, you take both prisoners and territory.

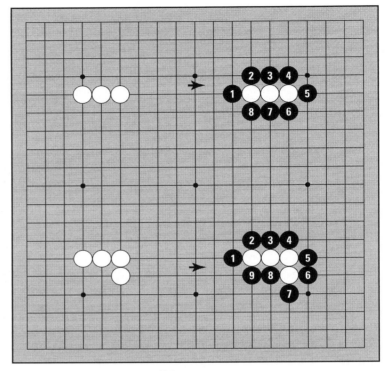

Diagram 10

TRY IT YOURSELF

Problem 1:

Both Black and White are in atari. Where can Black play to capture a stone?

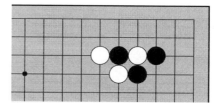

Problem 1

Problem 2:

What stones are in atari? Where is a good place for Black to play?

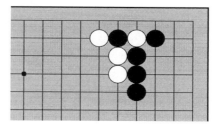

Problem 2

Problem 3:

Three black stones in the corner are in atari. Do you see any other stones in atari? Black can capture a stone blocking one of the liberties of his three stones. Where?

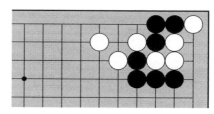

Problem 3

Problem 4:

Black has just played 1. What stones are in atari? Where is a good place for White to play?

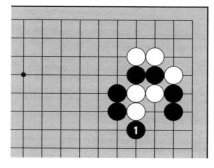

Problem 4

TRY IT YOURSELF

Problem 5:

White 1 puts the two black stones in atari. What can Black do?

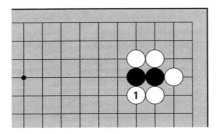

Problem 5

Problem 6:

Where do black stones need to be in order to capture the three white stones?

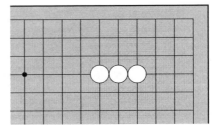

Problem 6

ANSWERS

Answer 1:

Black can capture a white stone at 1. If Black doesn't play at 1, White can capture a black stone by playing at A.

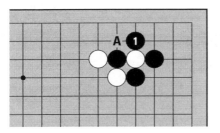

Answer 1

Answer 2:

The marked stones are in atari. Black can capture the white stone at 1.

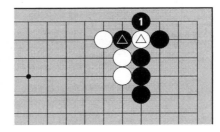

Answer 2

ANSWERS

Answer 3:

The white stone in the extreme corner blocking Black's liberty is also in atari. Black can capture it at 1. Since captured stones are removed immediately, Black's three stones are no longer in atari.

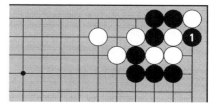

Answer 3

Answer 4:

The two black and three white marked stones are in atari. White can capture the two black stones with 1. After capturing, White's three stones are no longer in atari.

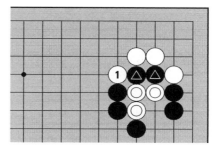

Answer 4

Answer 5:

Black can run by playing 1. Black is no longer in atari.

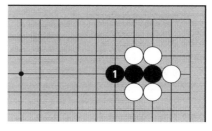

Answer 5

Answer 6:

To capture, Black needs to block all White's liberties. You don't need to block at the points marked A because they are not liberties.

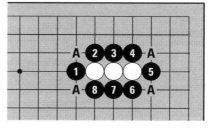

Answer 6

3

CONNECTING AND CUTTING

1. CONNECTING

Stones are **connected solidly** when they are on adjacent points connected by a line. This entails playing a stone on your own liberty.

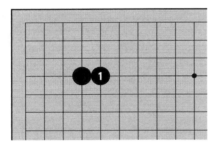

Diagram 1

Diagram 1:

Black 1 plays next to another black stone. These two stones are connected solidly.

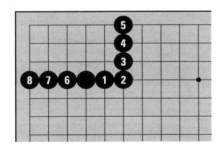

Diagram 2

Diagram 2:

Connections are the foundation of territory. The stones from 1 to 8 are all connected. Black has made territory in the corner.

Diagram 3:

Black's two stones are connected but White's are not. Where can White play to connect?

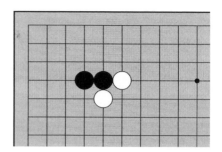

Diagram 3

Diagram 4:

When White plays 1, all her stones are now connected. If White does not connect, Black can cut these stones.

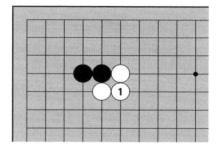

Diagram 4

Diagram 5:

If it is Black's turn, he can play at 1 to prevent the connection. These white stones are now cut. Stones that are cut act alone and have few liberties, so they are weak and are captured more easily.

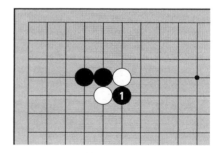

Diagram 5

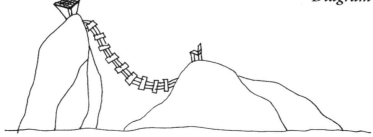

2.   CUTTING

If stones are prevented from connecting, they are said to be cut off from each other, or just **cut**. Cutting entails playing where your opponent needs to play to connect.

Diagram 6:

In the upper left, Black and White have similar shapes and four stones each. In the center, Black is connected and White is cut. In the lower right, White is connected and Black is cut. It makes a big difference who plays at 1: **connected stones are strong and cut stones are weak.**

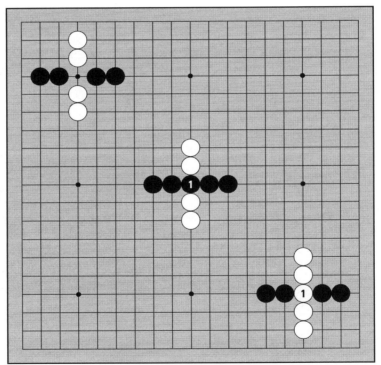

Diagram 6

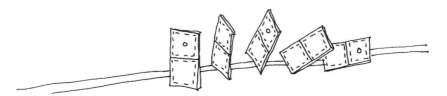

Diagram 7:

This is a common shape. All the black stones are connected but the white stones are not. If Black wants to cut, where should he play?

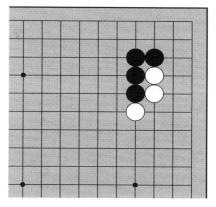

Diagram 7

Diagram 8:

If Black plays at 1, the white stones are now cut. White's position has become fragile.

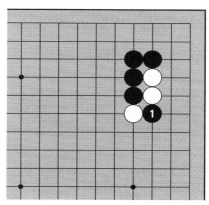

Diagram 8

Diagram 9:

If it is White's turn, she can play at 1. White is now connected.

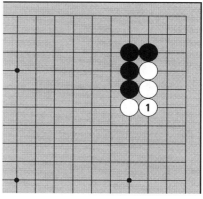

Diagram 9

3. THE DIAGONAL

When you play next to one of your stones on your own liberty (a line coming out from one of your stones), the stones are connected solidly. There are also indirect ways of connecting.

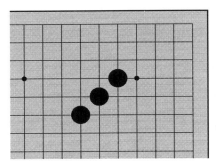

Diagram 10

Diagram 10:

Three black stones stand in a **diagonal**. Are these stones connected?

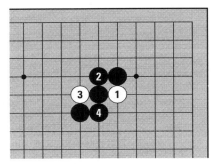

Diagram 11

Diagram 11:

Stones in a diagonal are not connected by lines, but if White plays 1, Black can play 2, and if White plays 3, Black can play 4, so White cannot cut. The diagonal is not a solid connection, but it cannot be cut because you and your opponent take turns.

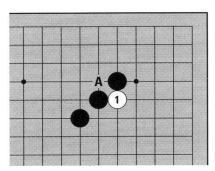

Diagram 12

Diagram 12:

When White plays 1, if Black plays elsewhere, White can cut by playing at A. When White plays 1, Black has to play to stay connected.

TRY IT YOURSELF

Problem 1:

One white stone is in atari. Can you connect all the white stones?

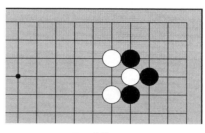

Problem 1

Problem 2:

Where can Black play to prevent White from cutting off a stone?

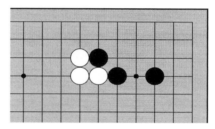

Problem 2

Problem 3:

What does White 1 mean and how should Black play?

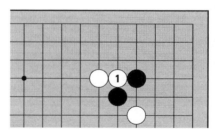

Problem 3

Problem 4:

How can Black connect the two black stones?

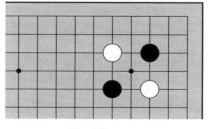

Problem 4

TRY IT YOURSELF

Problem 5:

White's turn to play. Where is Black's weak point?

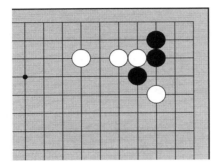

Problem 5

Problem 6:

If Black wants to cut off one white stone, where should he play?

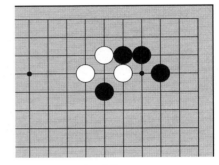

Problem 6

ANSWERS

Answer 1:

White 1 connects all her stones.

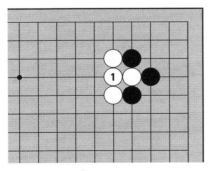

Answer 1

Answer 2:

Black 1 connects the weak point.

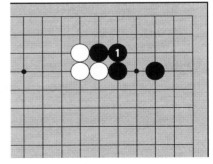

Answer 2

ANSWERS

Answer 3a:

If Black doesn't respond to 1, White can cut at A. This is dangerous for Black, so—

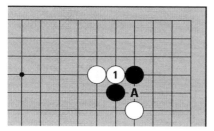

Answer 3a

Answer 3b:

Black should connect.

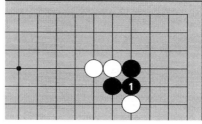

Answer 3b

Answer 4:

Black 1 connects diagonally.

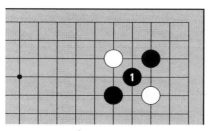

Answer 4

Answer 5:

White 1 cuts Black in two. Black is in a difficult situation.

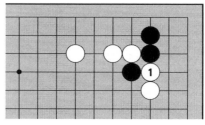

Answer 5

Answer 6:

Black 1 cuts off one white stone.

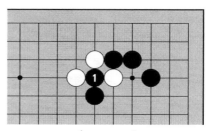

Answer 6

4

WHERE YOU CAN'T PLAY

For the most part, you can put your stones anywhere you like. Let's look at a place where you can't play.

1. THE POINT WITHOUT LIBERTIES

Diagram 1:

The shape on the left looks like the result when Black captures a stone. Can White play at A?

If White tries to play here, as on the right, White 1 doesn't have any liberties, so it is captured. Since captured stones are taken off the board, it looks like White didn't play but just gave Black a stone. You can't put a stone on a point without liberties.

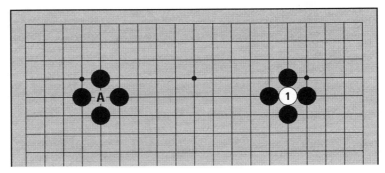

Diagram 1

Diagram 2:

Black 1 is not the same as White 1. Black 1 is connected to the other black stones and shares liberties with them.

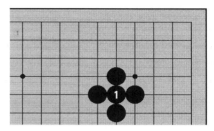

Diagram 2

Diagram 3:

Can White play 1?

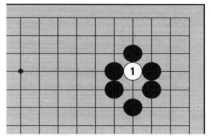

Diagram 3

Diagram 4:

White can play 1 because White's stone has a liberty at A. (Black can capture White 1 easily by playing at A, so White 1 has little meaning, but it still remains on the board.)

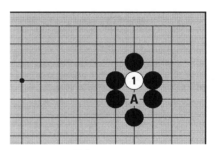

Diagram 4

Diagram 5:

How about White 1? This point has no liberties, so White cannot put a stone here.

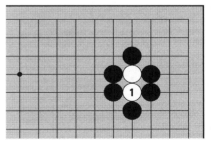

Diagram 5

2. GAINING LIBERTIES BY CAPTURING

If your opponent's stones are in atari you can capture them by blocking their last liberty. You gain liberties when taking out captured stones.

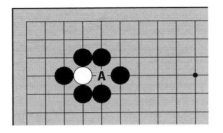

Diagram 6

Diagram 6:

In this position White cannot play at A, because this point has no liberties.

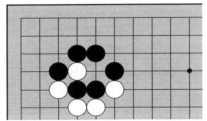

Diagram 7

Diagram 7:

Here, the two black stones at the bottom are in atari. Atari means the stones can be taken out on the next move.

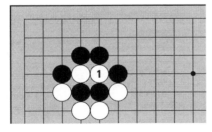

Diagram 8

Diagram 8:

In this case, the two black stones are captured by White 1.

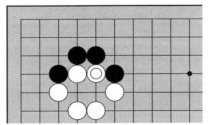

Diagram 9

Diagram 9:

This is the result. White could play at 1 in the previous diagram (the marked stone here) because Black was in atari and White gained additional liberties by capturing.

Diagram 10:

These eight white stones are connected and have one point of territory. Black cannot play in the center of this shape right now, because a stone there would be just taken out.

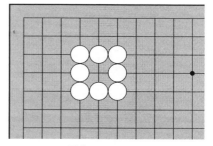

Diagram 10

Diagram 11:

But if Black blocks all the outside liberties of the white stones, White will be in atari.

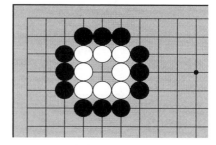

Diagram 11

Diagram 12:

Now Black can play at 1 and take out all the white stones. (Black cannot play at 1 if White has even one liberty on the outside, because White would not be in atari.)

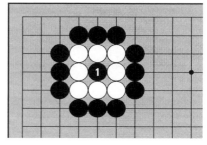

Diagram 12

Diagram 13:

This is the result.

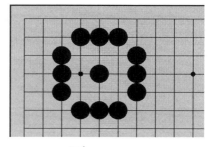

Diagram 13

TRY IT YOURSELF

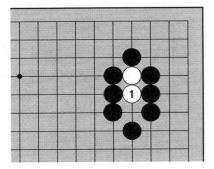

Problem 1

Problem 1:

Can White play 1?

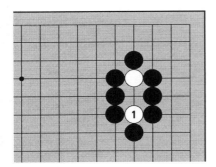

Problem 2

Problem 2:

Can White play 1?

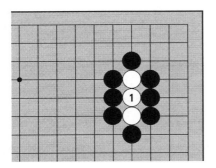

Problem 3

Problem 3:

Can White play 1?

TRY IT YOURSELF

Problem 4:

If White connects at 1, the three white stones will be in atari. If Black plays next at A, the three stones will be captured. Can White play 1?

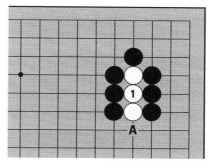

Problem 4

Problem 5:

Can White play 1?

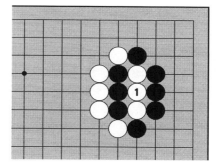

Problem 5

ANSWERS

Answer 1:

White can play 1 because these two stones have a liberty.

Answer 2:

White can play 1 because this stone has a liberty.

Answer 3:

White can't play 1 because these three stones have no liberties.

Answer 4:

White can play 1. It's suicidal but these stones do have a liberty at A.

Answer 5:

White can play 1. It looks like her three stones have no liberties, but here the three black stones are in atari, so White can gain liberties by capturing them.

LIFE AND DEATH

If you understand the principles behind capturing, you can "unpack" them to discover their consequences — stones that have no liberties are removed from the board, therefore you can't play on a point without liberties, unless you gain liberties by capturing. At the bottom of the suitcase are the logical conclusions of these principles: life and death.

Diagram 1:

If all the liberties of the two white stones are blocked, they will be captured. Even if White's stones have a point of territory, if all their outside liberties are blocked, they will be in atari and can be captured. But some stones cannot be captured.

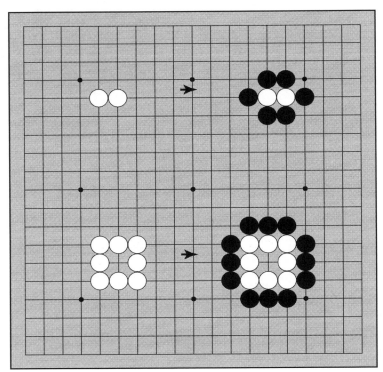

Diagram 1

1. LIFE

Diagram 2:

The black group of stones in the upper left corner has two separate points of territory. Even if all their outside liberties are blocked completely, White cannot capture these stones. For White to capture, the black stones first must be in atari. But these stones can never be placed in atari.

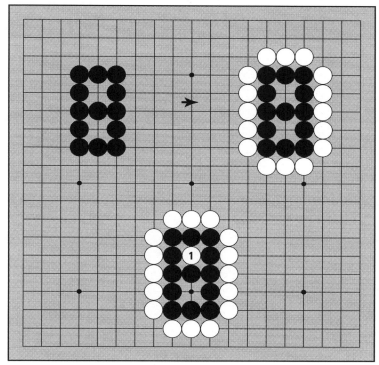

Diagram 2

Even after Black is surrounded completely, White cannot play 1, because a stone there is just taken off. Since you cannot play on a point without liberties, these black stones cannot be put in atari. Any group with at least two separate points of territory cannot be put in atari, and so cannot be captured. Stones which cannot be captured are **alive**.

Diagram 3:

Each of these black groups has two separate points of territory. Even though they are surrounded, they cannot be captured, so they are alive. It takes fewer stones to make two separate points of territory in the corners than on the sides or in the center, so it is easiest to live there.

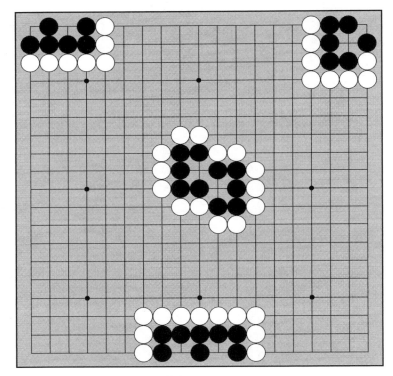

Diagram 3

2.   DEATH

Even if a group has two points of territory, if the two points are not separated, the group is not alive.

Diagram 4:

The black stones in the upper left corner have two points of territory, but the points are not separated. These stones can be captured.

To take out these stones, White can play at 1. This is possible because White 1 has a liberty. The black stones are now in atari, so they can be captured on the next move. White 1 is in atari also, so Black can capture it with 2, but after capturing his group is still in atari. Next White can capture all his stones with 3. Stones that can be captured are **dead**.

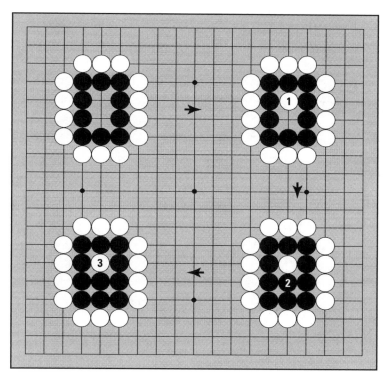

Diagram 4

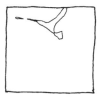

3. CONDITIONS FOR LIFE

Stones must have at least two separate points of territory for life. These two separate points are called **eyes** (*jip* in Korean, meaning "house," or *meh* in Japanese, meaning "eye"). Some shapes can make two eyes.

Diagram 5:

These black groups are surrounded and have only one eye. They can't live because they don't have enough room inside to make two eyes.

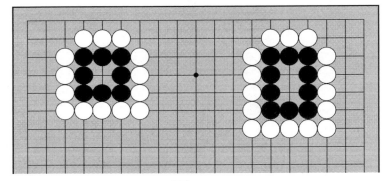

Diagram 5

Diagram 6:

The black group on the left has three points of territory in a straight line. If Black plays 1, as on the right, this group will have the two eyes necessary for life. If Black does not play 1, White can move in for the kill.

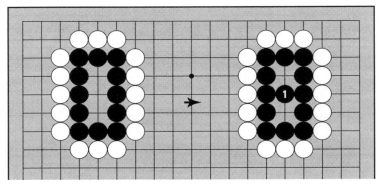

Diagram 6

Diagram 7:

If Black doesn't play at 1, White will play there. Now Black's group is dead. Black doesn't have a good move here, since any move he makes would just be putting his stones in atari. If White wants to take them out, she can play atari with 3. Black can capture the two white stones with 4, but this group still doesn't have two eyes. Finally, if White plays 5, Black is reduced to one liberty.

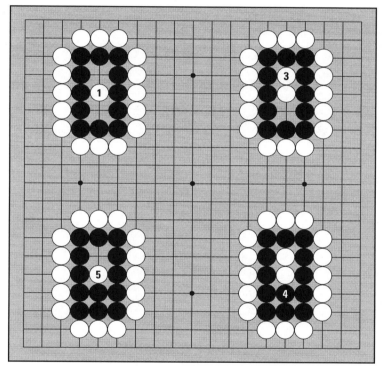

Diagram 7

Diagram 8:

Here Black has four points of territory in a straight line. If he plays at 1, he has two eyes, one of which is larger than the other. But even if Black doesn't play 1, this group is alive.

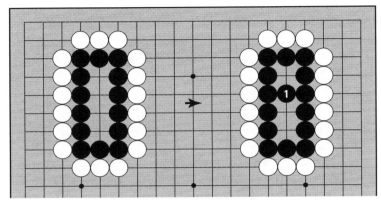

Diagram 8

Diagram 9:

If White tries to kill with 1, Black can make two eyes by blocking at 2 as on the right. When there are four points in a straight line, it is not necessary to spend an extra move to make two eyes. Even if White attacks, Black has enough room to live.

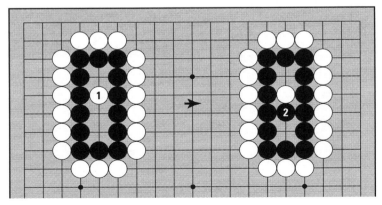

Diagram 9

4. FALSE EYES

A **false eye** looks like a real point of territory but it is not.

Diagram 10:

Black is surrounded. Are these stones alive or dead? It looks like Black has two eyes, but the three black stones at the bottom are not connected solidly to the main group.

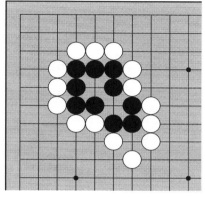

Diagram 10

Diagram 11:

If White plays 1, the three stones are in atari. If Black connects at 2, Black has only one eye. But if Black does not connect at 2—

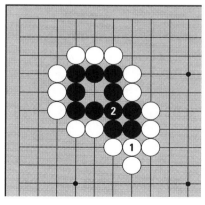

Diagram 11

Diagram 12:

White can capture at 3. Once again, Black has only one eye. That's why Black in *Diagram 10* is dead.

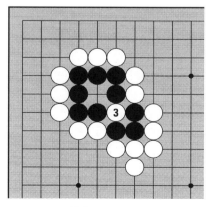

Diagram 12

Diagram 13:

The black group on the left does not have two eyes because Black ▲ is not connected solidly to the main group. In fact, this marked stone is in atari. On the right, the black group has one eye in the corner but the second "eye" is false. (If White plays at A, Black ▲ will be in atari.)

Neither of these groups can escape or make two eyes, so all these black stones are dead.

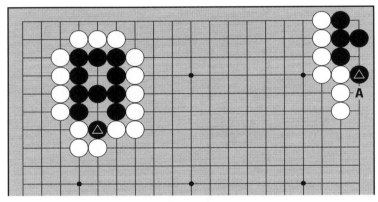

Diagram 13

5. A SPECIAL FORM OF LIFE

Stones must have two eyes to live, but in some unusual cases, Black and White can live together without two eyes.

Diagram 14:

The four black stones and three white stones are cut off and have no eyes. But these stones cannot capture or be captured by each other.

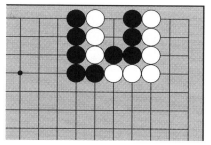

Diagram 14

Diagram 15:

If Black plays 1, his stones will be in atari, so next White can capture them.

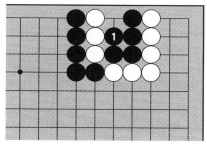

Diagram 15

Diagram 16:

But if White plays 1, her stones will be in atari, so next Black can capture. This is a mysterious shape in which the first person to play here is captured. Therefore, no one wants to play here, and since one doesn't have to, a local stalemate is the result.

This is called **dual life**. Dual life is called *seki* in Japanese and *beek* in Korean, meaning both sides have equal rights in an area and can't be captured. It's recommended that you avoid using the Japanese term, which means "offspring of a female canine" in Korean.

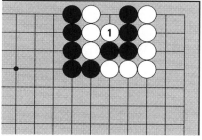

Diagram 16

TRY IT YOURSELF

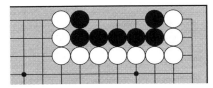

Problem 1:

Black is surrounded. Where should he play for life?

Problem 1

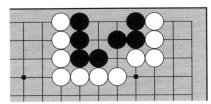

Problem 2:

If White wants to kill, where should she play?

Problem 2

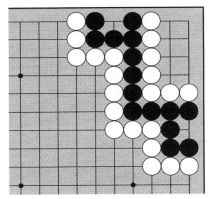

Problem 3:

Black is surrounded. Is he alive or dead?

Problem 3

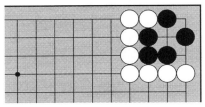

Problem 4:

Is the black group in the corner alive as it stands, or does Black need to play?

Problem 4

TRY IT YOURSELF

Problem 5:

Can White kill the black stones in the corner?

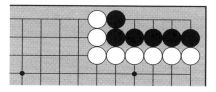

Problem 5

Problem 6:

The three white stones and the four black stones are cut off and neither has eyes. Where can Black play to make dual life?

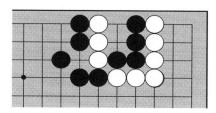

Problem 6

ANSWERS

Answer 1:

Black 1 lives by making two eyes.

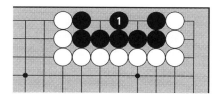

Answer 1

Answer 2:

If White plays 1, Black is dead.

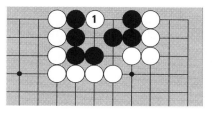

Answer 2

ANSWERS

Answer 3:

Black is alive. Black has one eye on the top and another eye on the other end of the group. It has two separate points of territory so it is alive.

Answer 4:

Black must play 1 to make an eye at A. If Black does not play 1, White can play there and A will become a false eye. (Notice the three black stones would be in atari if White played at 1.)

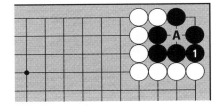

Answer 4

Answer 5:

White cannot kill. Four points in a straight line is alive as it stands.

Answer 6:

Black can make dual life by playing 1. Neither side can capture the other in this position.

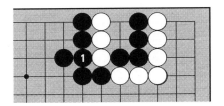

Answer 6

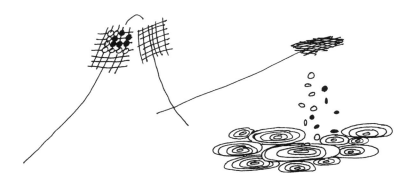

GO STRENGTH

Ability in Go is called **strength**. Go strength is distinguished by levels called **dan** (pronounced dahn), and **kyu** (Japanese) or **gup** (Korean). Although there is some variation in levels from country to country, we will use standard Korean rankings as a model.

After learning the rules of Go and playing one game, you are ranked 18 gup. As you improve, your level rises through 17 gup, 16 gup, etc., until you reach 1 gup. At this stage, you advance into the dan levels. The amateur levels range from 1 dan (entering level, called *shodan* in Japanese and *chodan* in Korean) to 6 dan (top level). The difference in levels is approximately one handicap stone. For example, if you take eight handicap stones from a 1 dan, you are approximately 8 gup.

There are about 700 professional Go players in the world today. Professionals are players who have advanced through the amateur ranks and then, by winning a special yearly national tournament held in China, Japan, and Korea, are awarded professional status. Pro levels are also measured in dan, ranging from 1 dan (entering level) to 9 dan (top level). The difference in these dan levels is too small for handicaps in professional competition.

Research indicates that the difference between top professionals and top amateurs is between two and three handicap stones. Amateurs also compete and teach like professionals do; "professional" is just a term indicating a kind of graduate degree in Go.

There are some other systems. For example, Westerners sometimes are ranked "20 kyu" or "30 kyu" in an attempt to make finer distinctions among beginners. Ranks can be confusing, but nothing to worry about—it's best not to get too hung up on ranks if you want to get strong quickly. Play at a rank or a handicap that offers a challenge for both players, and change when it is appropriate. Many people like playing a series of games with one opponent, changing the handicap after two, three, or more straight victories. This is called playing *kadoban* (Japanese) or *chisugochigi* (Korean).

If you study Volume 1, you will be able to play at around the 15 gup level. Volumes II and III in this series cover the ground from 15 to 12 gup. Try your best and you may reach the amateur dan level within a year or two.

6

KO

Ko is a special shape in which Black and White can capture each other repeatedly. The rule of ko is important because it allows the game to continue.

1. WHAT IS KO?

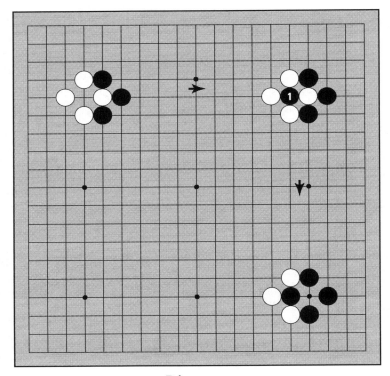

Diagram 1

Diagram 1:

In the upper left corner, the white stone is in atari, so Black can capture it with 1. The resulting shape is shown in the lower right corner. Now the black stone is in atari. If White captures it, we return to the original position. This could go on forever; in fact, the Japanese word *ko* means "eternity." Ko is called *pae* in Korean, meaning "no-man's point" (like the demilitarized zone).

2. THE RULE OF KO

When a stone captures in ko, it may not be captured immediately.

Diagram 2:

Black captures the white stone in ko. White may not capture Black 1 immediately. Once White has played a stone anywhere else on the board, she may return to the ko to capture Black 1.

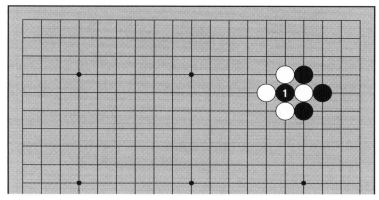

Diagram 2

Diagram 3:

White 2 has played away from the ko in response to Black's capture. If Black plays somewhere else (at 3 for example) instead of connecting his stone in ko, White may return to capture it with 4. Now Black may not capture White 4 immediately, but must play somewhere else first.

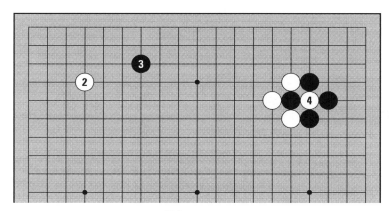

Diagram 3

TRY IT YOURSELF

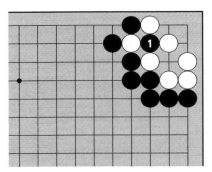

Problem 1

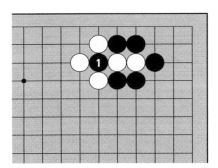

Problem 2

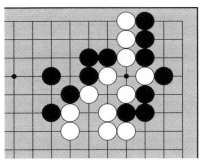

Problem 3

Problem 1:

Black 1 captures one white stone in ko. White wants to capture Black 1 but may not do so immediately. What does White have to do before capturing?

Problem 2:

Black 1 has captured two white stones. Can White capture Black 1 immediately?

Problem 3:

Can you find the stone in ko for Black to capture?

TRY IT YOURSELF

Problem 4:

White 1 captures one black stone in ko. Black wants to capture White 1 immediately but may not do so because of the rule of ko. Black must play somewhere else first. Can you think of a good place for Black to play, that is, a place where White will respond, so that Black can return to the ko? (Don't think too hard. Just try to find a place where Black can play that White should answer.)

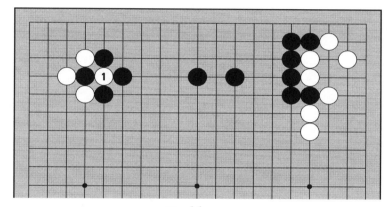

Problem 4

ANSWER

ANSWER 1:

White must play somewhere else, after which White may capture.

Answer 2:

White 2 can capture the black stone immediately because this shape is not ko. Notice White 2 is not in atari, so Black cannot capture it.

Answer 3:

Black 1 captures a stone in ko. Notice the three white stones on the top are being cut off.

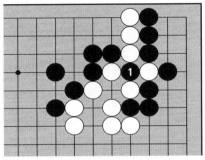

Answer 3

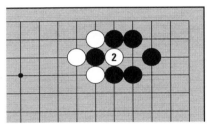

Answer 2

Answer 4:

Black can play atari at 1. If White connects at 2 to save the two stones, Black may return to capture the white stone in ko with 3. (Ko fighting will be explained in more detail in Part II.)

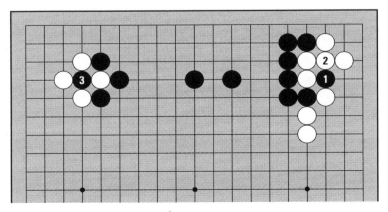

Answer 4

THE MANY NAMES OF GO

The game of Go has various other names. Go is called *Weiqi* in China. The Chinese character *wei* means "to surround." Players surround area to make territory or surround stones to capture them, so "the surrounding game" is an apt description. Go is also referred to by characters meaning "hand conversation" or "talking with the hands," since even people who don't speak the same language can communicate through Go. The first character can be read as "hand" or "stone," so another reading is "talking with stones."

As well as being an interesting amusement, Go is also believed by many to develop one's brain power and even build character. One certainly must use one's intellect to play Go, but one is also rewarded for awareness, a calm heart, and a sense of purpose. Even though it is not a physical sport, Go is categorized as a martial art because of the aspects of self-development involved. That's why Go is sometimes called "The Way of Go" or "The Teachings of Go" (*ki-do*).

Internationally, we use the Japanese pronunciation *go* because of the great effort the Japanese have made to popularize Go around the world. Koreans use their native word *baduk* instead of *go*.

7

TERRITORY

Territory is the space inside a wall of stones of the same color. It comes in all shapes and sizes.

Diagram 1:

Here are some different territories. In the upper left Black has two points of territory. In the upper right Black has eight points of territory. On the left side, White has an irregular shape with thirteen points of territory. White has twelve points of territory in the lower right.

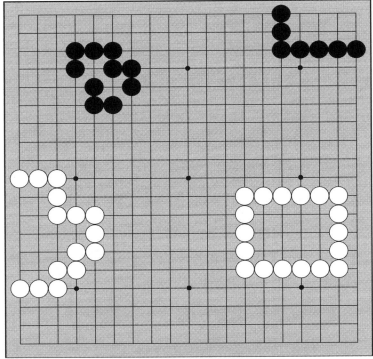

Diagram 1

1.   CONDITIONS FOR TERRITORY

For an area to become territory, the surrounding walls cannot have any weak points that can be assaulted successfully.

Diagram 2:

White punches through Black's wall with 1. This corner is not territory because Black's wall has been breached.

Diagram 3:

Black needs to protect the corner territory by blocking the gap with 1. White cannot mount a successful assault now, so this corner becomes Black's territory.

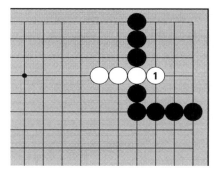

Diagram 2

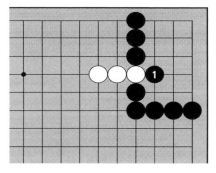

Diagram 3

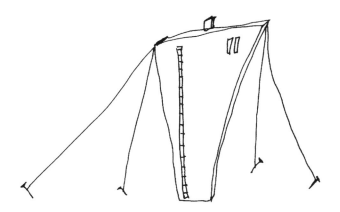

Diagram 4:

Black has surrounded a large territory comprising more than a fourth of the board. The walls have no weak points, but this territory is so big (100 points) that it has other problems.

Diagram 5:

If White **invades** at 1, Black will be in an awkward position. Attacking White 1 is difficult because the black stones are so far away. If Black cannot capture White 1, a lot of Black's territory will be destroyed.

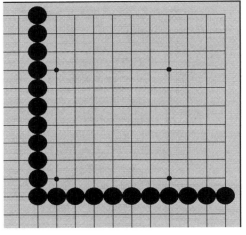

Diagram 4

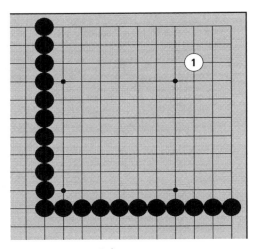

Diagram 5

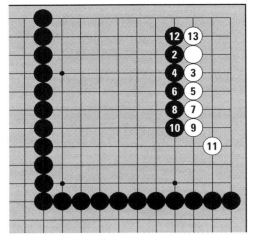

Diagram 6

Diagram 6:

If Black attacks at 2, White can play 3. In the sequence shown, Black continues the attack, but is unsuccessful. In fact, White makes about ten points of territory in the corner that used to be Black's territory.

Stake a claim to territory that you can control, that is, where your opponent cannot live easily inside it.

TRY IT YOURSELF

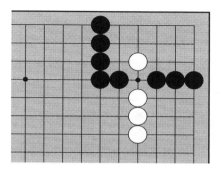

Problem 1

Problem 1:

Where can Black play to protect the corner territory?

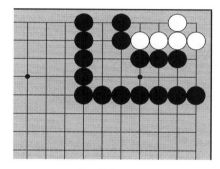

Problem 2

Problem 2:

This shape is the result of a white invasion. Black must kill the invading stones to keep the corner territory. How can Black do so?

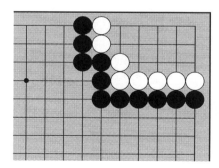

Problem 3

Problem 3:

White has surrounded the corner but it is not all territory yet. There is a weak point in White's wall. Where is it?

TRY IT YOURSELF

Problem 4:

Here are three territories with nine points each. How many stones are needed for making the territory in the center? On the side? In the corner? In order of efficiency, which areas are best for making territory?

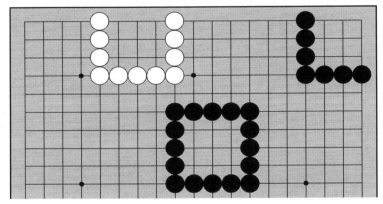

Problem 4

ANSWERS

Answer 1:

Black connects at 1, making a solid wall.

If Black does not play 1, White can cut through at 1. The corner is no longer Black's territory.

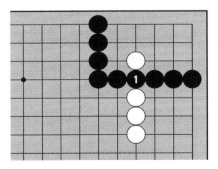

Answer 1a

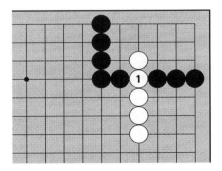

Answer 1b

ANSWER

Answer 2:

Black can play at 1. Now White cannot make two eyes (two separate points of territory). Since White can be captured, White is dead, and Black keeps the corner.

If Black does not play 1, White 1 makes two eyes. White cannot be captured, so White is alive. Black's territory has been considerably reduced by the invasion.

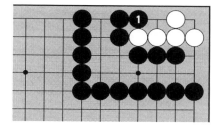

Answer 2a

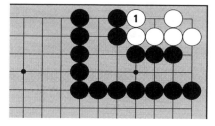

Answer 2b

Answer 3:

White needs to connect at 1 to make a perfect wall.

If White does not play 1, Black 1 perforates the wall, and some of White's territory is lost.

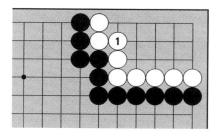

Answer 3a

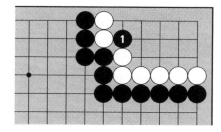

Answer 3b

Answer 4:

To make the same number of points, you need sixteen stones in the center, eleven on the side, and seven in the corner. The most efficient place to make territory is the corner because there are two "walls" already. On the side, one "wall" is constructed for you. In the center, territory must be protected on all four sides.

HANDICAP GO

Go has a convenient handicapping system whereby players of different strengths can still play an interesting game. In a handicap game, the weaker player places stones on the board before the game begins. Handicaps range from two to nine stones. They are placed on the star points according to this chart:

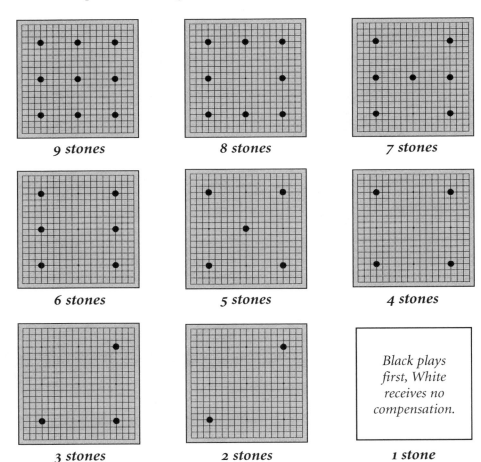

9 stones   *8 stones*   *7 stones*

6 stones   *5 stones*   *4 stones*

3 stones   *2 stones*   *1 stone*

Black plays first, White receives no compensation.

In an even game, Black has an advantage by playing first. To minimize this advantage, White receives **compensation** (*komi* in Japanese and *dom* in Korean). Compensation is added to White's total territory at the end of the game. The standard compensation is 6¹/₂ points. The half point avoids ties.

PLAYING GO ON THE INTERNET

You can get a game anytime online on a Go server. A good one to try is the Kiseido Go Server at www.gokgs.com. You can watch or play as a guest, or easily register for a free account.

The Beginner's Room, or the Computer Go Room, is a good place to start playing Go online. You can click on a game being offered, or offer a game yourself. When you are setting up a game, it will ask the rules to be used, the size of the grid, the handicap and compensation (komi), and the time control. The defaults of an even game on a 19x19 grid with 6.5 komi are the most common settings. Rule sets are very similar and since only very rarely does a rules question come up, and the server will score the game for you, you don't have to worry too much if it is not on the default Japanese rule set, you can just jump in and start playing.

There are a number of different time controls in Go. Traditional time control is called byo-yomi, which means "second counting" in Japanese. In byo-yomi, each player receives a certain amount of main time. After the main time is used up, the player enters byo-yomi. In byo-yomi, you have a certain number of seconds to play your move; if you go over, you use up a byo-yomi period. If you use up all your byo-yomi periods, you lose on time. For example, the default time control is 30 minutes of main time, with five byo-yomi periods of 30 seconds each. That means you have 30 minutes on your clock; after you use 30 minutes, you must play each move within 30 seconds. If you go over 30 seconds five times, you lose on time. The server keeps track and counts down your seconds for you and how many byo-yomi periods you've used. It's a good idea to play with a time control that you feel comfortable with, as it's very easy in Go to get lost in thought and not spend your time productively without a little prodding. Byo-yomi is good to start with because it is easiest to use to manage your time while playing.

If you are playing "free" games, you don't have to worry about a rank. If you want to get a rank on the server, you can register your account and play ranked games -- depending on your results, the server will set your rank. Don't worry too much about your rank when you are starting out though -- they change too quickly in the beginning to mean very much.

A REAL GAME

The following is a real game on a 13 x 13 board. Watch how stones are captured, how territory is made, and how the winner is decided.

Game Record 1 (1-2):

Black plays first. Black 1 is in the upper right corner. White 2 occupies the lower left corner. Usually one takes up a position in the corners on the third or fourth line from the edge first, because it strikes a good balance between offense and defense.

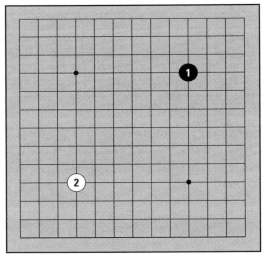

Game Record 1 (1-2)

Game Record 2 (3-6):

Black plays in the lower right corner with 3, and White takes the last remaining corner with 4. Next Black makes a claim to the side with 5. In the beginning, you can make a good position by playing your stones somewhat sparsely in important areas. Next White begins surrounding the upper left corner with 6.

Game Record 3 (7-12):

Black makes inroads into the upper side and extends the territorial framework of the upper right corner with 7. White 8 approaches the lower right corner. Open hostilities start when Black attaches on top with 9 and White tries to circle around from underneath with 10. Black blocks at 11, and White 12 puts a stone in atari. Where will Black play next?

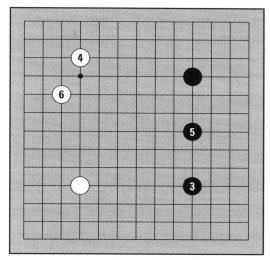

Game Record 2 (3-6)

Game Record 4 (13-15):

Black connects at 13. If Black does not connect, White will capture at 13. White connects a weak point on top at 14 and Black 15 cuts at the bottom.

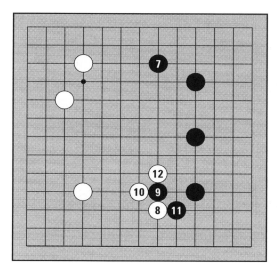

Game Record 3 (7-12)

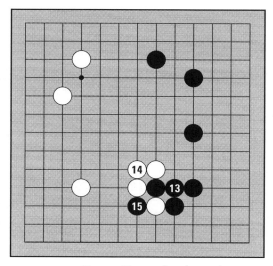

Game Record 4 (13-15)

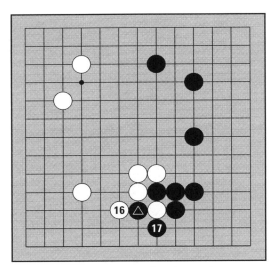

Game Record 5 (16-17)

Game Record 5 (16-17):

White 16 puts Black ⬤ in atari, but Black can capture first at 17. Black puts the white prisoner in his bowl lid.

Game Record 6 (18-20):

White 18 puts a black stone in atari. Black doesn't connect, but tries to cut off White 18 instead. White captures with 20.

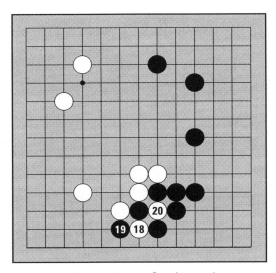

Game Record 6 (18-20)

Game Record 7 (21-22):

White ◎ is in atari, but it has just captured in ko. Black may not capture it immediately, so he plays at 21. White responds at 22, so now Black may return to capture White ◎.

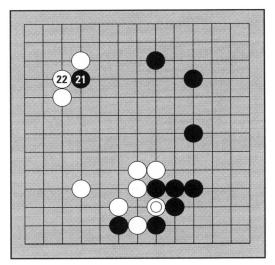

Game Record 7 (21-22)

Game Record 8 (23-25):

Black **takes the ko** with 23. Now White may not capture Black 23 immediately, so she plays somewhere else with 24. Black responds at 25.

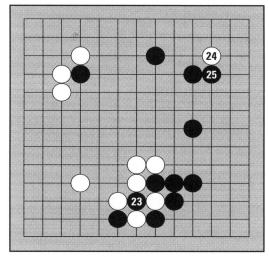

Game Record 8 (23-25)

Game Record 9 (26-27):

Since White has played somewhere else, White may return to capture the black stone in ko with 26. Black also must play somewhere else before capturing, so he blocks at the top at 27. If White responds, Black can take the ko again.

Game Record 10 (28-31):

White does not respond, but **connects the ko** at 28. Now the ko fight on the bottom is finished. White has **won the ko**, but Black makes a strong position at the top with 29 and 31.

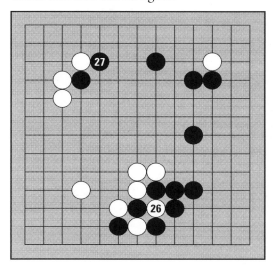

Game Record 9 (26-27)

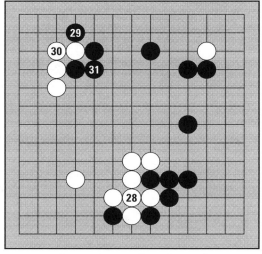

Game Record 10 (28-31)

Game Record 11 (32-36):

White turns her attention to the upper right corner with 32. White means to live here and so must make a minimum of two eyes. When Black blocks at 33, White extends potential eye space with 34 and connects with 36.

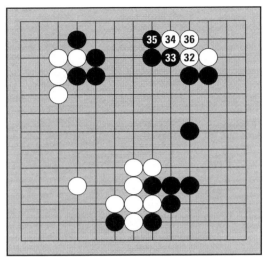

Game Record 11 (32-36)

Game Record 13 (43-47):

Black jumps into the white area on the left side with 43. White 44 defends the corner territory. Black runs with a diagonal at 45. White tries to enclose these stones with 46 but Black comes out at 47.

Game Record 12 (37-42):

Black tries to kill White's group, starting by coming straight down at 37. To be successful, he must prevent White from making two eyes. But when Black connects at 41, White, after connecting at 42, can now make two eyes no matter what Black does. Try to confirm for yourself that White is alive now due to Black's ineffective attack.

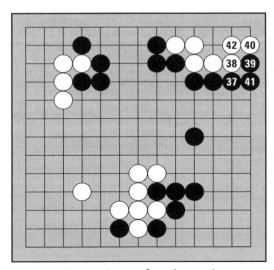

Game Record 12 (37-42)

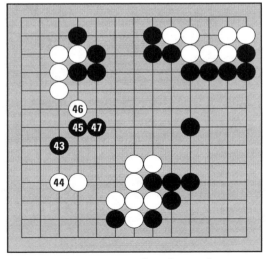

Game Record 13 (43-47)

Game Record 14 (48-53):

White follows with 48 so Black runs again at 49. If surrounded, Black cannot make two eyes on the inside, so these stones must run out and link up to the secure stones on the right side in the sequence to 53.

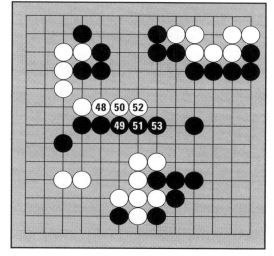

Game Record 14 (48-53)

Game Record 15 (54-59):

White blocks at 54, protecting the territory in the upper left corner. Black connects at 55. White wants to destroy the territory on the right side, so she invades at 56. Black attacks with 57 and 59, intending to kill.

Game Record 16 (60-68):

White's invading stones are surrounded, so they need at least two separate points of territory to avoid capture. In Gospeak we say White cannot run, so she must make two eyes to live inside.

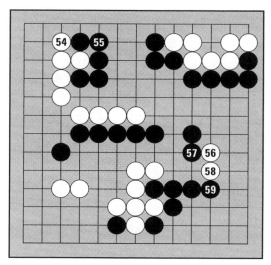

Game Record 15 (54-59)

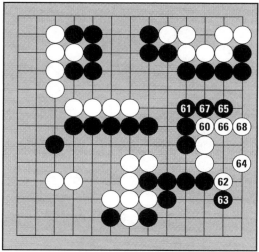

Game Record 16 (60-68)

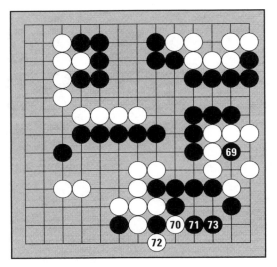

Game Record 17 (69-73)

Game Record 17 (69-73):

White could live by playing at 69, but unfortunately for these stones, it is Black's turn. Black plays at 69, preventing White from making two eyes, so the invading stones die. White switches to 70, capturing one stone. Black protects strongly at 73.

Game Record 18 (74-78):

White was killed on the right side, so now White threatens Black's indirect connection at 74. Black plays coolly at 75 and 77. If Black did not connect at 77, White could cut off two stones by playing there.

Game Record 19 (79-84):

Black 79 makes another important connection. White protects the corner territory by blocking at 80. Black 81 protects the territory on top. What is the meaning of White 84?

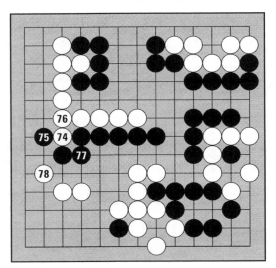

Game Record 18 (74-78)

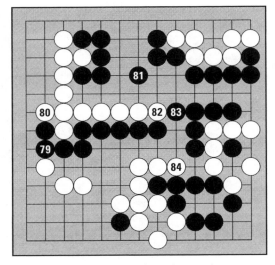

Game Record 19 (79-84)

Game Record 20 (85-89):

Black must play at 85, otherwise the seven dead stones on the right can connect to the secure stones on the left. When White plays at 86, Black connects at 87. This is also very important because White is threatening to cut off the big group on the left side.

Now the major fighting is finished. The **endgame** starts with 88 and 89.

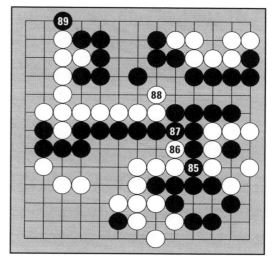

Game Record 20 (85-89)

Game Record 21 (90-95):

White 90 puts a stone in atari, so Black connects at 91. Next White connects at 92. Black plays the **hane** (a Japanese term meaning a kind of "quick turn") with 93. The "hane-block-connect" on the first line is one of the more common techniques of the endgame.

White blocks at 94 and Black connects at 95. The territories are beginning to take their final forms.

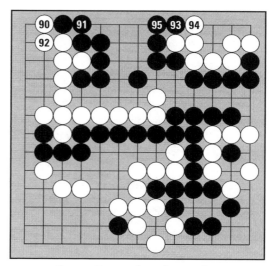

Game Record 21 (90-95)

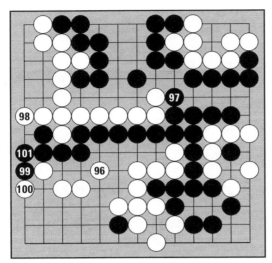

Game Record 22 (96-101)

Game Record 22 (96-101):

White 96 expands the territory in the lower left a little more. Black 97 seals off his right side. White 98 completes the upper left corner's wall. Next Black plays the hane at 99 in the lower left, White blocks, and Black connects.

Game Record 23 (102-108):

White prevents the formation of one point of territory with 102 and Black connects all his stones with 103. He puts the finishing touch on the top territory with 105 in response to 104. White plays the hane at 106, Black blocks, and White connects.

Game Record 24 (109-112):

Black plays atari at 109 and White connects at 110. If White does not connect, Black can capture one stone and break through her wall. Black plays 111 and White blocks at 112.

Now there are no places on the board where territory can be reduced or enlarged, so both players passed.

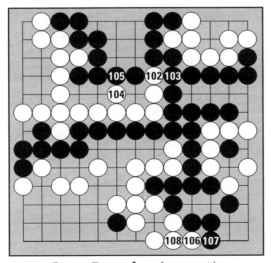

Game Record 23 (102-108)

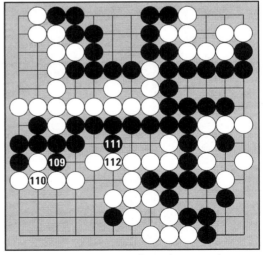

Game Record 24 (109-112)

Diagram 1:

At this stage, there are some things we should do in order to count and see who won more easily. First, we have to deal with the places marked X. Nobody can make territory in these areas. These are called **neutral points** (*dame* in Japanese, and *gongbae* in Korean).

In some rule sets, the game is not officially over until all the neutral points are filled, so players take turns filling them before passing. In the common-use Japanese and Korean rule sets though we pass even if there are some neutral points left, and filling them in is part of the counting and scoring.

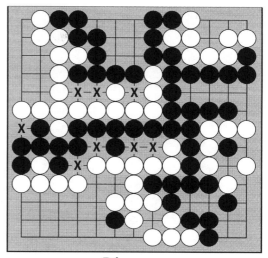

Diagram 1

Diagram 2:

Black and White fill in the neutral points. This clarifies what is territory and what is not. After all the neutral points have been filled, dead stones are removed.

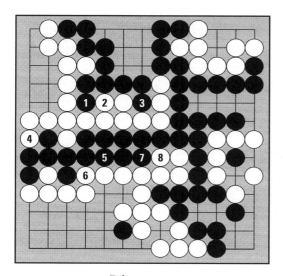

Diagram 2

Diagram 3:

The dead stones are Black ▲ and White ◎. Dead stones are taken out at the end of the game. It is not necessary to play extra moves in order to capture them. For example, White need not play A and B to remove Black ▲ at this stage.

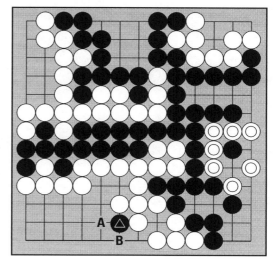

Diagram 3

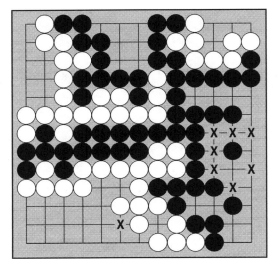

Diagram 4

Diagram 4:

This is the result after the dead stones at X have been removed. The dead stones are prisoners and join their fellow prisoners in the bowl lids. White has four prisoners, and Black has nine.

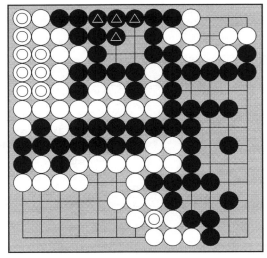

Diagram 5

Diagram 5:

Black fills in white territory with white prisoners; White fills in black territory with black prisoners. Each dead or captured stone reduces your opponent's territory by one point. After the territories are filled in with prisoners, the territories can be arranged for easy counting.

Diagram 6:

Moving stones around does not change the territory count as long as you do not touch the borders. Arrange the territories to make rectangular shapes for easy counting.

White has 20 + 4 = 24 points. Black has 25 points. Black has won by one point.

You are now ready to play Go.

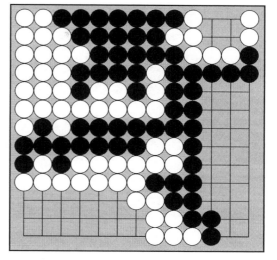

Diagram 6

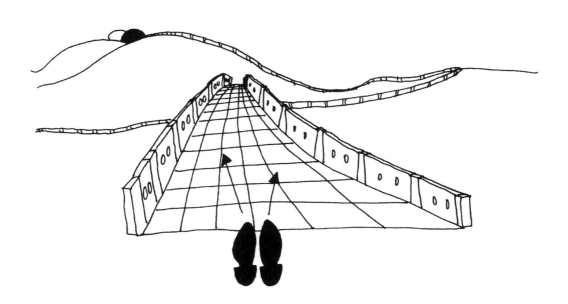

Go Stars

Cho Hoon-hyun

B. 3/10/53, Korea. 1 dan 1962, 9 dan 1982. Studied in Japan as a disciple of Segoe Kensaku 9 dan. Returned to Korea for obligatory military service in his teens, and has remained ever since. Held every Korean title for many years, and several world championships.

Cho Hoon-hyun's other claim to Go greatness lies in his teaching of Go star Lee Chang-ho 9 dan.

Suh Bong-soo

B. 2/1/53, Korea. 1 dan 1970, 9 dan 1986. Won the prized title of *Myungin* at 18 and held it for five straight years. A home-grown "solution to Cho Hoon-hyun," Suh was Cho's only rival in the 80s. His victory in the Ing Cup made Suh, who was known as the "Korean number-two player," a World Champion.

GO STARS

Yu Chang-hyuk

B. 4/25/66, Seoul. 1 dan 1984, 9 dan 1996. Fujitsu World Champion 1993. The subject of a two-volume biography at the age of 28. A true Horatio Alger story, Yu was the fifth of seven children of a poor family, who went on to fame and fortune by studying Go books at home. Yu emerged from the ranks of the top amateurs as the first and leading player of the Go generation dubbed by the media the "new wave."

Lee Chang-ho

B. 7/29/75, Korea. 1 dan 1986, 9 dan 1996. A disciple of Cho Hoon-hyun. Guinness world record holder for youngest person to win a Go title (at age 14). In a sport where most players peak in their 30s, Lee at 19 held more titles (13) than any other player. Lee's youth and amazing skill has raised interest in Go to new heights. In a survey in Korea, he was ranked the eighth-most-recognized person in the world.

Photos: Hankook Kiwon

GO STARS

JAPANESE STARS

Cho Chi-hoon — B. 6/20/56, Seoul. Nephew of Cho Nam-chul 9 dan, who founded the Hankook Kiwon (Korean Go Association). Entered Kitani School in Japan in 1962. 1 dan 1968, 9 dan 1981. 1983 held top four titles (*Kisei, Meijin, Honinbo, Judan*) at the same time. Only player to have won all seven Japanese top titles. Called Cho Chikun in Japanese.

Kato Masao — B. 5/15/47, Fukuoka, Japan. Kitani disciple. 1 dan 1964, 9 dan 1978. Won fourteen titles from 1976-1980. Known as the "Killer" for his penchant for spectacular captures.

Kobayashi Koichi — B. 9/10/52, Asahikawa, Japan. Kitani disciple. 1 dan 1967, 9 dan 1979. Considered by many to be the top Japanese player of the 1990s. Married to Kitani's daughter, Reiko 6 dan, who passed away in 1996. *Kisei* seven, *Meijin* four consecutive years. First player to top $1 million annually in playing fees.

Otake Hideo — B. 5/12/42, Kitakyushu, Japan. Kitani disciple. 1 dan 1956, 9 dan 1970. *Meijin* 1975 and three more times. *Gosei* 1980-85. In all, 39 titles.

Rin Kaiho — B. 5/8/42, Shanghai. A disciple of Wu Ch'ing-yuan (called Go Seigen in Japanese), who is considered by many to be the greatest player of the 20th century; Rin Kaiho is Go Seigen's foremost disciple. 1 dan 1955, 9 dan 1967. *Meijin* 1965 and seven times thereafter. *Honinbo* five times.

Takemiya Masaki — B. 1/1/51, Tokyo. Kitani disciple. 1 dan 1965, 9 dan 1977. Invented the "Outer Space Style," a large-scale center strategy. *Honinbo* six times.

CHINESE STARS

Nie Wei-ping — B. 8/17/52, Hubei Province, China. Chinese Champion 1975 and five more times. A national hero, called the "Iron Goalkeeper" for preventing Japanese victories in the Japan-China Super-Go matches.

Rui Nai-wei — B. 12/28/63, Shanghai, currently living in Tokyo. First woman 9 dan. Bohae Cup World Women's Champion 1995 and 1996. Semi-finalist in Ing Cup 1992. Married to Jiang Zhu-jiu 9 dan.

GO IN THE U.S.A.

In 1907, a famous chess master named Edward Lasker discovered Go in Berlin, watching Japanese students play in their leisure hours. At first skeptical that it had the depth of chess, he quickly became entranced. In one of his books, he wrote: "My friends to whom I showed the game...soon preferred it, like myself, to all other games they knew." These early Go players founded the New York Go Club in 1927, and in 1935, the American Go Association (AGA), which today has grown to over 100 member clubs. Contact information for Go clubs in North America can be found at the AGA's website at www.usgo.org.

There are dozens of local and regional tournaments, culminating in the yearly U.S. Go Congress, where the U.S. Open, as well as numerous other events, take place. You can join the approximately 1,500 active members of the AGA and participate in AGA tournaments for a small membership fee.

The U.S. lags behind Asia and Europe in Go population, but a number of players have achieved very respectable results in international amateur competition, and the first three professional players born outside of Asia are American:

Michael Redmond

B. 5/25/63, California. Disciple of Oeda Yusuke 9 dan. 1 dan 1981, 9 dan 2000 from the Nihon Ki-in (Japan Go Association). Highest ranked American-born player.

Janice Kim

B. 10/21/69, Illinois. Disciple of Jeong Soo-hyun 9 dan. 1 dan 1987, 3 dan 2003 from the Hankook Kiwon (Korea Baduk Association).

James Kerwin

B. 11/1/46, Minnesota. Disciple of Iwamoto Kaoru 9 dan. 1 dan 1978 from the Nihon Ki-in. Teaches the annual Hollyhock Go retreat and Winter Go Workshop.

PART 2

BASIC TECHNIQUES

*In Part I, you learned the fundamentals.
As you play, you may find that although
your objectives may be simple, they are not
always easy to accomplish.*

*In Part II, you will learn basic techniques,
and how to use them in your own games.*

9

CAPTURING TECHNIQUES

Capturing is profitable — it not only increases your territory, it reduces your opponent's territory. Everybody wants to capture, but it is not easy. When you try to capture, your opponent can run.

Diagram 1:

On the left, Black 1 puts one white stone in atari. If Black plays next, he can capture. But since it is White's turn, she can come out at 2. White now has three liberties, so capturing becomes more difficult. Even if Black blocks a liberty at 3, White can stay one step ahead with 4. It looks like capturing is hopeless now.

Is it only by luck or miscalculation that stones are captured? Not really. There are stones you can capture if you learn some basic techniques.

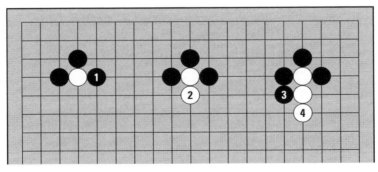

Diagram 1

1. DOUBLE ATARI

You can capture stones by making a double threat.

Diagram 2:

Where can Black play to put both white stones in atari at once?

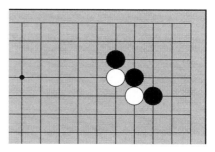

Diagram 2

Diagram 3:

When Black plays at 1, both white stones are in atari at the same time. They are said to be in **double atari**. When you play double atari, you can capture one side or the other.

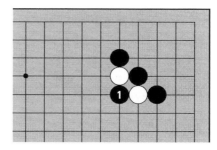

Diagram 3

Diagram 4:

If White runs at 2, Black 3 captures the other stone. If White runs at 3, Black can capture at 2.

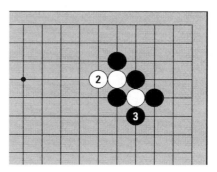

Diagram 4

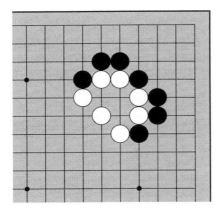

Diagram 5

Diagram 5:

This shape has a vital point for double atari. Try to find it.

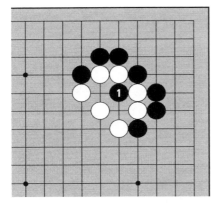

Diagram 6

Diagram 6:

Black 1 is the vital point. The two white stones on the top and the two on the side are in atari at the same time. Black can capture one side or the other.

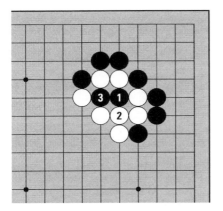

Diagram 7

Diagram 7:

If White connects the two stones on the side with 2, Black can capture the two on top with 3.

Diagram 8:

But if White connects the two stones on the top, Black can capture the two on the side.

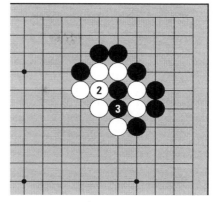

Diagram 8

Diagram 9:

This is the result of *Diagram 8*. The shape that results from capturing two stones looks like an aerial view of a turtle, so it is called the **turtle back**.

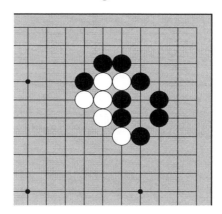

Diagram 9

2.　PUSHING TOWARDS THE EDGE

Another way to capture stones is by pushing them towards the edge.

Diagram 10:

There is one black stone and one white stone on the first line. Where can Black play to capture?

Diagram 11:

Black 1 is not good because White can run into the center with 2. Black can't capture this way.

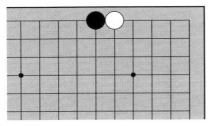

Diagram 10

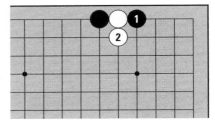

Diagram 11

Diagram 12:

Pushing White towards the edge with Black 1 is correct.

Diagram 13:

If White tries to run at 2, Black can play atari at 3. In the sequence from 4 to 8, White continues to run and Black follows, threatening to capture with each move. Finally White is captured in the corner. A stone on the first line is captured easily because it is running down a dead-end alley.

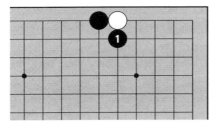

Diagram 12

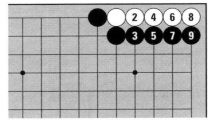

Diagram 13

Diagram 14:

Now the white stone is on the second line. How can Black capture it?

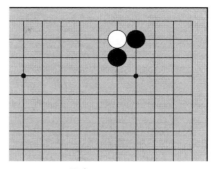

Diagram 14

Diagram 15:

If Black tries to capture with 1, White can run at 2. Black has made a mistake by pushing in the wrong direction.

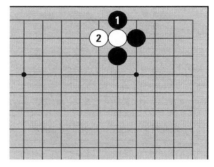

Diagram 15

Diagram 16:

Pushing White towards the edge is correct. Even if White plays 2, White is trapped. Black can play atari with 3.

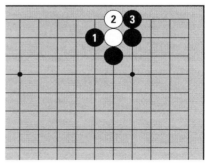

Diagram 16

Diagram 17:

How can Black capture White 1?

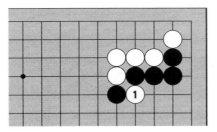

Diagram 17

Diagram 18:

Black 1 is a mistake. White runs into the center with 2.

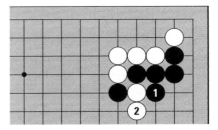

Diagram 18

Diagram 19:

Black should push White towards the edge with 1. Now White has problems.

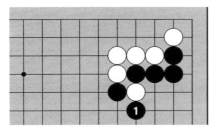

Diagram 19

Diagram 20:

Even if White runs at 2, 4, and 6, Black finally traps these stones on the first line. Often you may capture stones by pushing them to the edge, where they can be trapped.

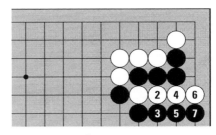

Diagram 20

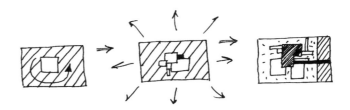

Diagram 21:

Black 1 cuts off two stones. How should White play here?

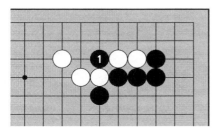

Diagram 21

Diagram 22:

Playing White 1 is a mistake this time, because Black can come down at 2.

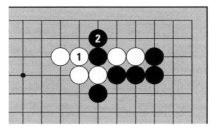

Diagram 22

Diagram 23:

If White tries to capture with 3, Black can capture first. Before trying to capture stones, you should consider your opponent's response. This is called **reading**.

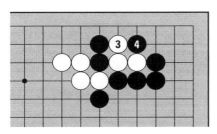

Diagram 23

Diagram 24:

Surrounding Black with White 1 is correct. Even if Black plays at A, he is still in atari.

In this case, pushing towards the edge is not a good idea, but usually it is the correct way.

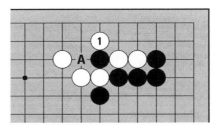

Diagram 24

3. THE LADDER

The ladder is a most interesting capturing technique.

Diagram 25:

Here we have one white stone menaced by three black stones. Black can capture.

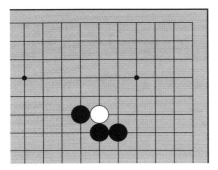

Diagram 25

Diagram 26:

Black 1 doesn't work because White can run at 2, gaining additional liberties.

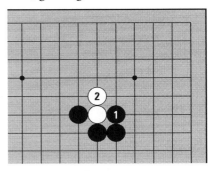

Diagram 26

Diagram 27:

Black 1 makes best use of Black ▲. Let's see what happens if White tries to run.

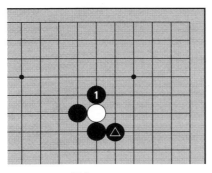

Diagram 27

Diagram 28:

If White runs at 2, Black can play atari in front at 3. If White then runs at 4, Black can play atari in front again at 5. Using this technique, Black pushes these stones towards the edge. Eventually White will be captured on the first line. Playing atari in front and trapping on the edge is called the **ladder**.

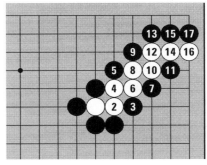

Diagram 28

Diagram 29:

This is the result after the white stones have been captured in the ladder. Black is very pleased.

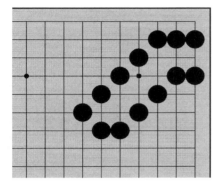

Diagram 29

Diagram 30:

If Black plays at 1, he can capture. It's a bad idea for White to run at A, since it only increases the loss.

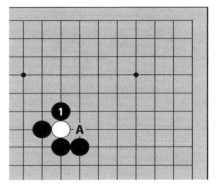

Diagram 30

Diagram 31:

Black plays at 1, hoping to catch a stone in a ladder. This time there is a white stone in the way. What happens in this case?

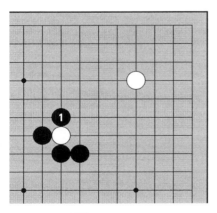

Diagram 31

Diagram 32:

White runs at 2, and Black plays the ladder sequence. But when White connects to White ◎, Black can no longer play atari in front. When there is an opposing stone in the way, you suffer a lot of damage by using the ladder technique.

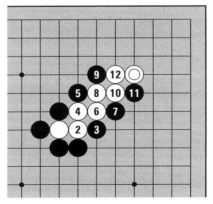

Diagram 32

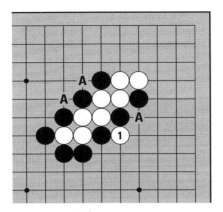

Diagram 33

Diagram 33:

After White has escaped, next she may play double atari at 1. In fact, White can play double atari at all the points marked A. Many weak points are created in the ladder, so don't use the ladder technique if your opponent's stones lie along the ladder's path.

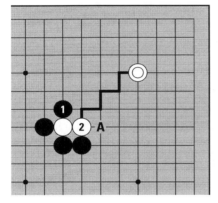

Diagram 34

Diagram 34:

If Black plays at 1, because of the marked stone, White can run at 2. If Black continues to try to capture in a ladder at A, White can escape by following the thick line. If there is a white stone near this line, Black should not use the ladder technique. White ◎ is called a **ladder breaker**.

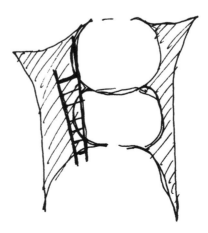

4. THE NET

So far, capturing techniques have involved reducing the liberties of enemy stones. There are also indirect methods.

Diagram 35:

The black stones are cut by White ◎. Can Black capture this stone?

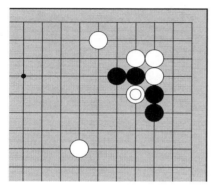

Diagram 35

Diagram 36:

If Black tries the ladder with 1, White can escape because there is a ladder breaker.

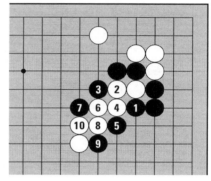

Diagram 36

Diagram 37:

In this position, Black can snare White with 1. White cannot escape.

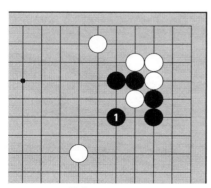

Diagram 37

Diagram 38:

Even if White pushes out at 2, Black can block at 3. Next if White plays at A, Black can capture at B. This technique is called the **net**.

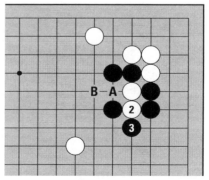

Diagram 38

Diagram 39:

Black can capture two stones in a net. How?

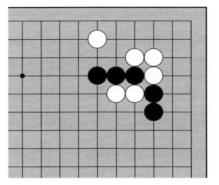

Diagram 39

Diagram 40:

If Black plays at 1, White can escape at 2, so Black can't snare White this way.

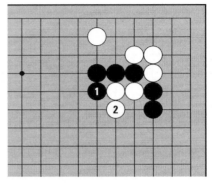

Diagram 40

Diagram 41:

Black 1 is the key point of the net. The two stones can't escape.

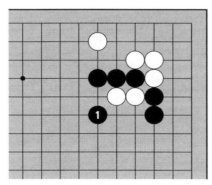

Diagram 41

Diagram 42:

If White tries to push out with 2, Black can block at 3. Next, if White plays at 4, Black can block again at 5, and White is in atari. White shouldn't try to save stones caught in a net like this, because it only increases the loss.

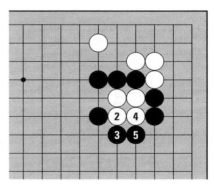

Diagram 42

5. THE SNAPBACK

There is a capturing technique in which you put your own stone in atari. It's like baiting a trap.

Diagram 43:

If Black wants to capture two stones, where should Black play?

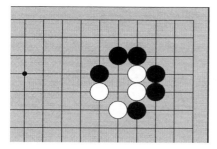

Diagram 43

Diagram 44:

Black plays atari at 1. This looks like walking into the tiger's mouth, but it's the white stones that are as good as captured.

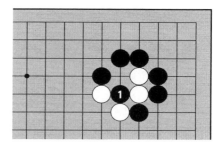

Diagram 44

Diagram 45:

If White plays at 2, the black stone is captured, but now three white stones are in atari.

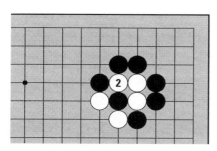

Diagram 45

Diagram 46:

Black can capture them at 3. It doesn't do any good to take the bait if caught in the **snapback**.

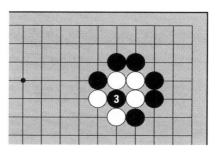

Diagram 46

Diagram 47:

Four white stones on the right can be captured in a snapback. It looks like White has territory, but actually there's a weak point.

Diagram 48:

Black can play at 1. This cut is the vital point of the snapback. Black 1 puts the four stones in atari. Black 1 is in atari as well.

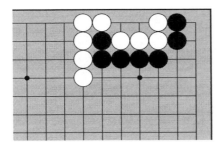

Diagram 47

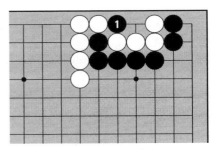

Diagram 48

Diagram 49:

White can capture with 2, but after she captures, five white stones are in atari.

Diagram 50:

Black can capture them at 3. Once Black plays 1, the four stones are caught in a snapback and cannot be saved.

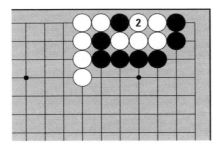

Diagram 49

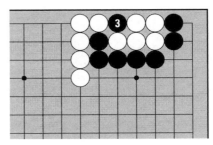

Diagram 50

6. THE PIN

You can capture stones when your opponent cannot connect all their weak points. Stones in atari that cannot connect are said to be **pinned** (*chok-chok-soo*, "chopping off the tail" in Korean, and *oi-otoshi*, "chasing and fleeing" in Japanese). Sometimes you can take advantage of weak points and pin directly. Other times you'll need the **throw-in** technique to reveal weak points.

Diagram 51:

White has two weak points at A and B. Black can take advantage of them to capture two stones. How?

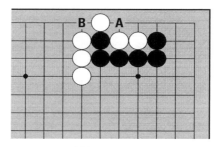

Diagram 51

Diagram 52:

Black can play atari at 1. White needs to connect at A to prevent Black from playing there and capturing two stones, but—

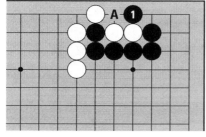

Diagram 52

Diagram 53:

If White connects at 2, Black can capture four stones at 3. White didn't have time to connect both weak points, so the two stones could not be saved.

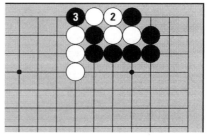

Diagram 53

Diagram 54:

How can Black take advantage of White's weak points to pin three stones?

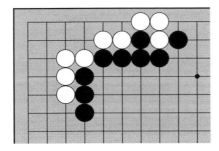

Diagram 54

Diagram 55:

Black plays atari at 1. If White connects at 2, she will leave a big weak point.

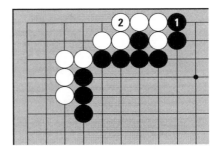

Diagram 55

Diagram 56:

Black can cut off six stones at 3. White is in atari now and cannot escape.

When Black threatens to capture at 1 in *Diagram 55,* White shouldn't connect at 2. If White tries to save the three stones, six stones will die.

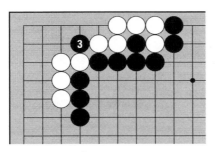

Diagram 56

Diagram 57:

If it's White's turn and she wants to save the three stones, she'll have to connect one of the weak points at 1. Then if Black plays atari at 2, she can connect at 3 with no problem.

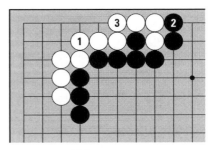

Diagram 57

Diagram 58:

Here, Black can capture three stones.

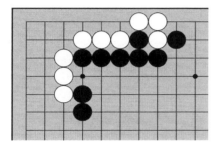

Diagram 58

Diagram 59:

In this case, if Black plays at 1, White can connect at 2. If Black cuts at 3, White is not in atari and so has time to capture the cutting stone with 4.

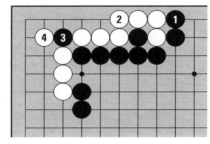

Diagram 59

Diagram 60:

Here, Black should throw in a stone at 1. The three white stones are in atari. Black 1 is in atari as well, so White can capture it with 2.

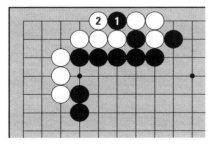

Diagram 60

Diagram 61:

Now Black can play at 3. The three stones are pinned. White shouldn't connect at 4, since Black can then capture eight stones by cutting at 5. With the throw-in, Black sacrificed one stone in order to reduce White's liberties, revealing weak points in White's position.

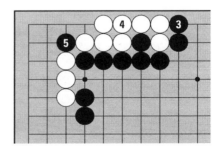

Diagram 61

Diagram 62:

This is a famous shape called the **crane's nest**. Black can capture three stones.

Diagram 63:

Black plays at the center with 1. This is the key point.

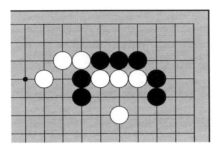

Diagram 62

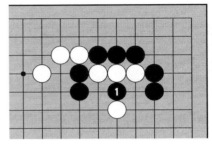

Diagram 63

Diagram 64:

If White tries to push out with 2, Black blocks at 3. Now four white stones are in atari.

Diagram 65:

If White captures one stone with 4, Black 5 puts White in atari, pinning five stones. (If White connects at the original Black 1, all seven white stones will be in atari and Black can capture.) This means that when Black plays at the center of the crane's nest, White can't save the three stones.

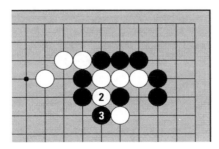

Diagram 64

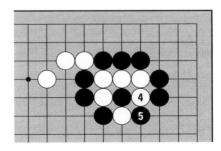

Diagram 65

TRY IT YOURSELF

Problem 1:

One black stone is cut off. If it wants to escape Black will have to capture the cutting stone. How can he do so?

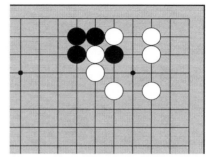

Problem 1

Problem 2:

There is a weak point in White's wall. Try to capture one white stone by making a double threat.

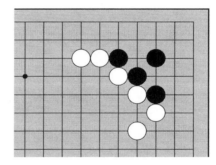

Problem 2

Problem 3:

How can Black capture the marked stone?

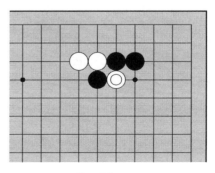

Problem 3

TRY IT YOURSELF

Problem 4:

If Black plays 1, does the ladder work?

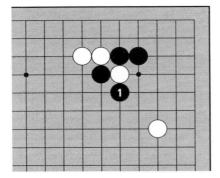

Problem 4

Problem 5:

Is there any way for Black to capture the marked stone?

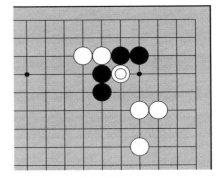

Problem 5

Problem 6:

It looks like Black is surrounded in the corner but White has a weak point. Where can Black play?

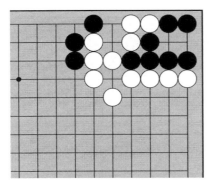

Problem 6

Problem 7:

Black can use White's weak points to capture some stones. Where can Black play?

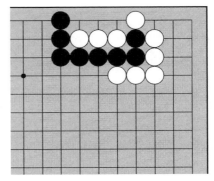

Problem 7

ANSWERS

Answer 1:

Black 1, pushing White towards the edge, is correct. White can't escape — if White A, Black B.

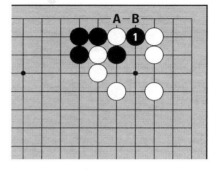

Answer 1

Answer 2:

Black 1 puts White in double atari.

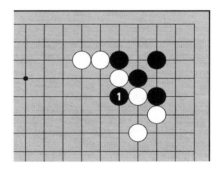

Answer 2

Answer 3:

Black plays 1. If White tries to run at 2, Black can capture by playing the ladder sequence.

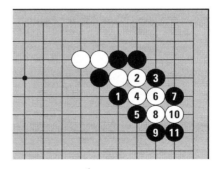

Answer 3

ANSWERS

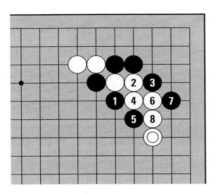

Answer 4

Answer 4:

White ◎ is a ladder breaker. If Black tries to capture anyway with 1 to 7, White can escape by connecting at 8.

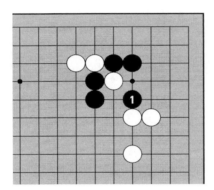

Answer 5

Answer 5:

The net of Black 1 is the only way to capture. White can't escape.

ANSWERS

Answer 6a:

Black 1 is the vital point for catching three stones in a snapback.

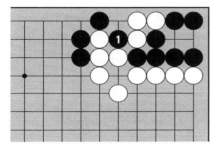

Answer 6a

Answer 6b:

If White captures Black 1 with 2, Black can capture four stones with 3 (at Black ●).

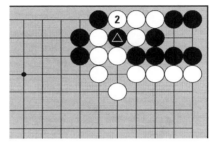

Answer 6b

Answer 7a:

The throw-in of Black 1 is the key. White can capture Black 1 but—

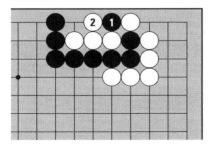

Answer 7a

Answer 7b:

Black can pin four stones with 3. (If White connects at A, Black captures at B.)

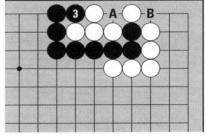

Answer 7b

10

CONNECTING TECHNIQUES

It is important to keep your stones connected. When connected, stones can work as a unit to surround territory, but when cut, it's work just to save them. There are many ways to connect stones.

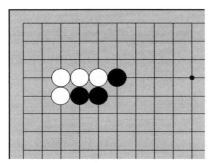

Diagram 1

1. THE TIGER'S MOUTH

Diagram 1:

White's stones are all connected but Black's are not. Black can be cut.

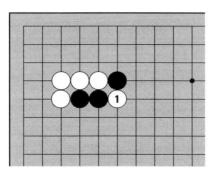

Diagram 2

Diagram 2:

If White plays at 1, Black is cut in two. How can Black protect against this cut?

Diagram 3:

Black can connect at 1. This is a solid connection. There are also other ways to connect.

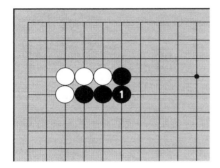

Diagram 3

Diagram 4:

Black 1 here is also a connection. Three stones in a "V" shape is called the **tiger's mouth**. (Some people call this the "hanging connection.") If White tries to cut by playing in the tiger's mouth, what will happen?

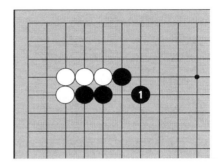

Diagram 4

Diagram 5:

If White cuts at 2, Black 3 can capture the stone. Playing in the tiger's mouth is suicidal. White can't cut here, so Black is connected.

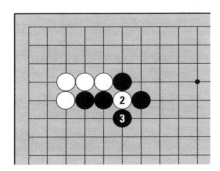

Diagram 5

Diagram 6:

Black 1 is also a tiger's mouth connection. You can solidly connect in only one place, but you can make a tiger's mouth connection in two places. In some cases, one needs to connect with the tiger's mouth.

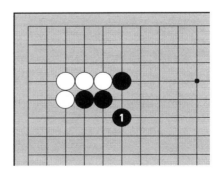

Diagram 6

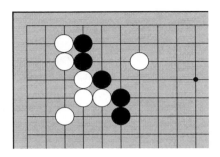

Diagram 7

Diagram 7:

These black stones have cutting points. Where can Black play to connect?

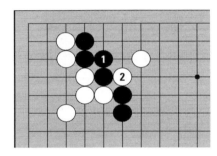

Diagram 8

Diagram 8:

If Black connects at 1, White can cut at 2.

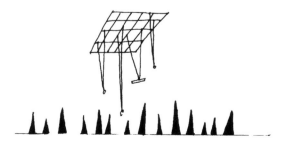

Diagram 9:

How about connecting at Black 1? White can still cut, this time at 2. If Black plays at 3, White can capture two stones with 4.

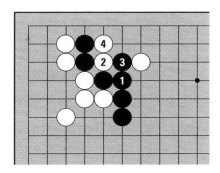

Diagram 9

Diagram 10:

When White cuts at 2, if Black plays at 3 here, White can connect at 4, and the black stones are still cut. In this shape, Black can't connect both weak points at the same time with a solid connection.

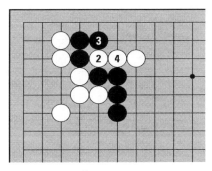

Diagram 10

Diagram 11:

Black can connect at 1 with a tiger's mouth. If White cuts on either side, Black can capture the cutting stone. Black 1 connects both weak points at the same time.

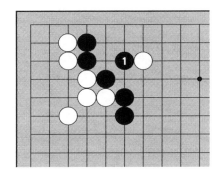

Diagram 11

2. THE KNIGHT'S MOVE

Diagram 12:

The four black stones are not connected. How can Black connect the weak point at A?

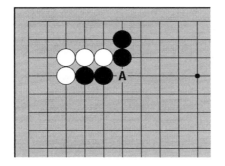

Diagram 12

Diagram 13:

Black can connect solidly at 1, or make a tiger's mouth connection at A or B, but there is another way.

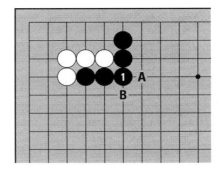

Diagram 13

Diagram 14:

Black 1 also connects.

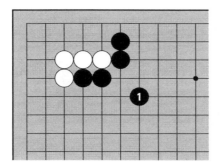

Diagram 14

Diagram 15:

If White cuts at 2, Black can push the cutting stone towards the edge in the sequence to 9. The cut here is a slow form of suicide.

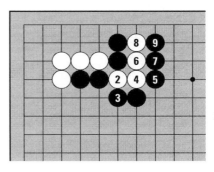

Diagram 15

Diagram 16:

Black 1 is also a connection. If White cuts, once again Black can capture the cutting stone.

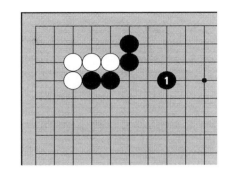

Diagram 16

Diagram 17:

Black captures in the sequence to 9. Black △ is an advanced connecting technique in which Black has to anticipate where a stone is needed if White cuts. This is another example of reading.

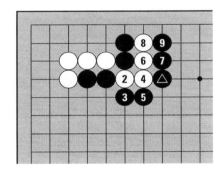

Diagram 17

Diagram 18:

Black 1 is called the **knight's move**. (The Japanese call this *keima* meaning "knight," but the Koreans call it *nar-il-ja* meaning "day," because it looks like the Chinese character for day.) Here, there are two stones that have a knight's move relationship with Black 1: Black ▲ and Black ⚫. A stone at A would also be a knight's move because of its relationship with Black ⚫. The knight's move is used in many contexts. Connecting using the knight's move is a difficult technique, so just be aware of it for now.

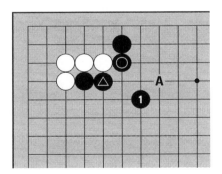

Diagram 18

3. THE BAMBOO JOINT

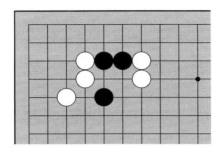

Diagram 19

Diagram 19:

The two black stones are not quite connected to the other black stone.

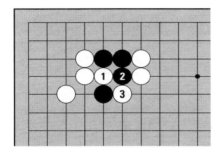

Diagram 20

Diagram 20:

White can cut at 1. Even if Black pushes out at 2, White can cut at 3, so Black wants to protect this cutting point.

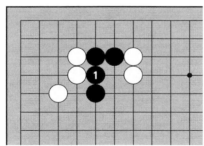

Diagram 21

Diagram 21:

If Black plays at 1, Black is connected, but there is a better way.

Diagram 22:

Black 1 here is a good way to connect.

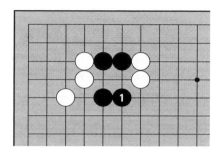

Diagram 22

Diagram 23:

If White tries to cut at 2, Black can connect at 3. If White tries to cut at 3, Black can connect at 2.

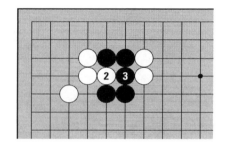

Diagram 23

Diagram 24:

Black 1 makes the shape known as the **bamboo joint**, where two pairs of stones are separated by a point. This shape is as good as connected. Why is Black 1 better than a play at A? It's better for moving out into the center.

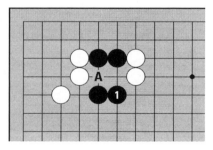

Diagram 24

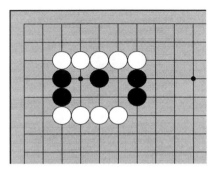

Diagram 25

Diagram 25:

How can you connect all the black stones?

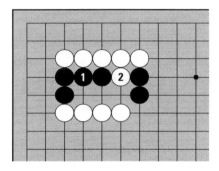

Diagram 26

Diagram 26:

If Black connects at 1, White can cut at 2. If Black connects at 2, White can cut at 1.

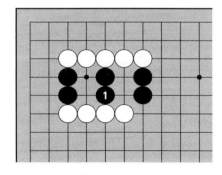

Diagram 27

Diagram 27:

In this case, the bamboo joint of Black 1 is the only way to connect. White cannot cut any of these stones.

4. CROSSING UNDER

Diagram 28:

The three black stones in the corner are in danger. If Black doesn't connect to the left side, Black is surrounded in the corner without two eyes. How can Black connect?

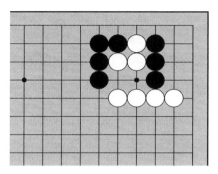

Diagram 28

Diagram 29:

Black 1 connects the two groups of stones. Black has **crossed under** White.

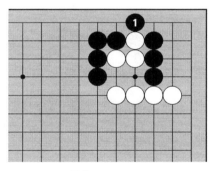

Diagram 29

Diagram 30:

If White cuts at 2, Black can capture at 3. If White cuts at A, Black can capture at B.

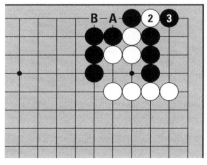

Diagram 30

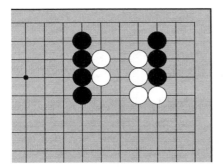

Diagram 31:

How can Black connect the stones on the left to the ones on the right?

Diagram 31

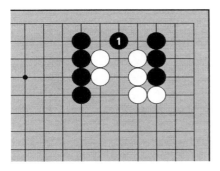

Diagram 32:

Black 1 here crosses under the white stones.

Diagram 32

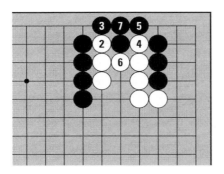

Diagram 33:

If White pushes in at 2, Black can cross under at 3. Next if White pushes in at 4, Black can cross under at 5. If White plays atari at 6, Black can connect safely at 7.

Diagram 33

TRY IT YOURSELF

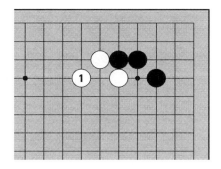

Problem 1

Problem 1:

White has played the tiger's mouth at 1. Can Black cut?

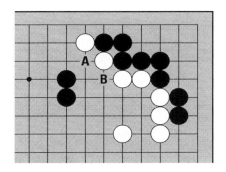

Problem 2

Problem 2:

White has cutting points at A and B. Where can White play to protect both weak points at the same time?

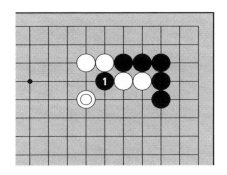

Problem 3

Problem 3:

When White protected the cut with White ◎, Black cut anyway at 1. This is a reckless move. Where can White play?

TRY IT YOURSELF

Problem 4:

White read that the knight's move of 1 would protect the weak point. Black cut anyway at 2. How can White capture this stone?

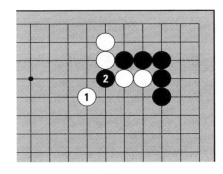

Problem 4

Problem 5:

To connect all the black stones, where should Black play?

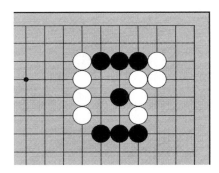

Problem 5

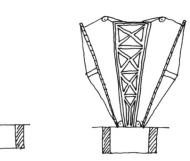

ANSWERS

Answer 1:

Black can't cut. If Black plays at 1, White can capture at 2.

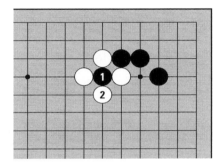

Answer 1

Answer 2a:

White can connect at 1, protecting both cutting points at the same time.

Answer 2b:

If White connects solidly at 1, Black can cut at 2.

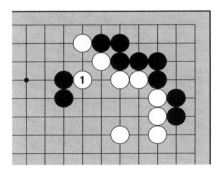

Answer 2a

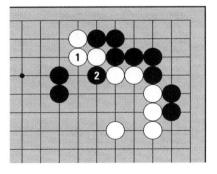

Answer 2b

ANSWERS

Answer 3:

White can capture the cutting stone easily at 2. If Black tries to escape at A, White can capture at B.

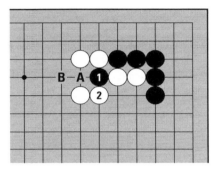

Answer 3

Answer 4a:

White can capture the cutting stone by pushing it towards the edge in the sequence from 1 to 7.

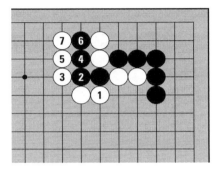

Answer 4a

Answer 4b:

White can also capture with the sequence from 1 to 9, in a ladder. Black can't cut here.

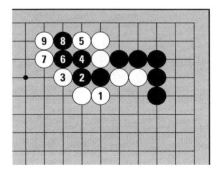

Answer 4b

Answer 4c:

White shouldn't play 1 on this side, however, since Black can capture two stones.

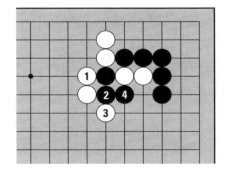

Answer 4c

ANSWERS

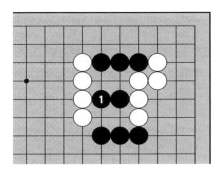

Answer 5

Answer 5:

The bamboo joint at Black 1 is the only connecting move.

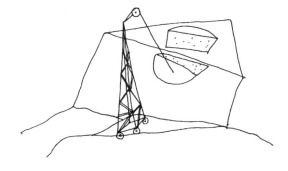

GO FOR KIDS

K ids as young as 3 or 4 are capable of learning about Go. Just drawing pictures with the stones on the board, and watching adults or older kids playing, is enough to spark their natural curiosity and imagination. They should be supervised at all times, though, because the stones look edible. Once the appeal of eating the stones has passed, kids seem to learn Go at an extraordinary rate. They often rapidly outpace adults and can reach professional levels as early as age eleven. Not only do kids learn Go with great ease, but many believe that learning it may increase a child's IQ or learning potential.

At first, kids (or adults, for that matter) may not understand all the information presented. Don't worry about it. The spirit of Go is in creative, not "correct," play. Do keep the focus on fun and sportsmanship. Generally speaking, kids are better at tactics than strategy. Try to let them excel at their natural strengths. Although it is difficult at times, the less said the better: let them see the consequences of their moves and decide for themselves if the moves are good or bad. Many people try to guide a child through a game or play illogically in an effort to let a child win, not realizing the uncertainty and confusion this may cause. Children are natural-born Go players. Let them do their own thing, don't do too much, and prepare to be amazed.

Kids are welcome at tournaments and there are also special tournaments just for them. The Michael Redmond Cup, the U.S. Go Congress, and the World Youth Championship are some of the opportunities to meet other children from around the world and visit interesting places. Support is also available to form a Go club in your area or provide equipment for your school. Visit the American Go Association's website at **www.usgo.org** for more information.

Photo by Hankook Kiwon

GO ETIQUETTE

In Asia, Go is a very mannered game. In fact, many people do not consider it a game at all, but an art. Gamesmanship is not an option. Go etiquette is functional and straightforward, and has a tendency to improve your play. The six keys are:

1. Have good manners even if your opponent does not.

2. Before beginning, players greet each other, usually by bowing.

3. Be calm. Nervous habits make you nervous.

4. Play confidently. Make the best of mistakes.

5. Try to be a gracious winner and a graceful loser.

6. Always put the stones away and thank your opponent before leaving.

Safety tip: Don't comment on games while they are being played.

The famous retirement game played in 1936 between Honinbo Shusai (on the right) and Kitani Minoru, which became the subject of Nobel prize-winning author Kawabata Yasunari's book, The Master of Go.

Life and Death Techniques

1. The Center

Diagram 1:

In the upper left, Black has three points of territory. Since he is surrounded, he must make two eyes to live. If he doesn't make two eyes, White can kill by playing 1 at the center of his territory.

Dead stones are helpless to avoid capture. If White wants to take these stones off the board, White can play 2. If Black tries to thwart this plan by capturing at 3, White can play in at 2 again and Black will be in atari.

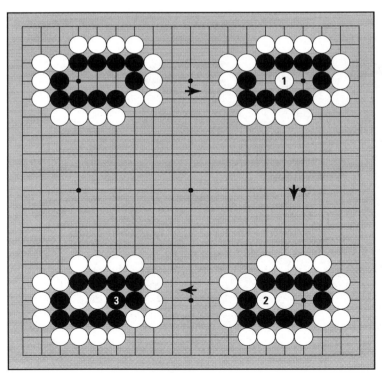

Diagram 1

Diagram 2:

The three black groups have all been deprived of two eyes by White's play at the center of Black's territory. Black had to make two separate points of territory by playing at 1 first.

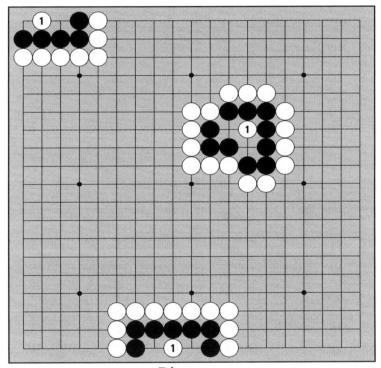

Diagram 2

2. EYE SHAPES

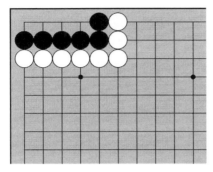

Diagram 3

Diagram 3:

Here Black has four points of territory in a straight line. In this shape, even if Black doesn't play first, he can live. Try to confirm for yourself that no matter where White plays, Black can make two eyes.

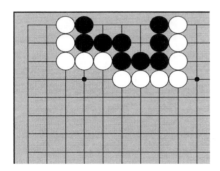

Diagram 4

Diagram 4:

This is another case in which Black has four points of territory and is alive without playing. Neither this black group nor the one above has a definite center point.

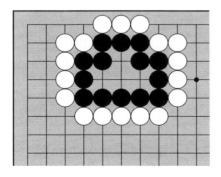

Diagram 5

Diagram 5:

This black group, however, is not alive yet.

Diagram 6:

Black can be killed by a play at the center of his territory.

Diagram 7:

If White wants to take these stones out, she can just start filling in liberties. With 3, Black is in atari. Black can try to prevent capture by capturing at 4, but it doesn't help.

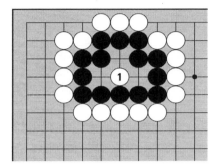

Diagram 6

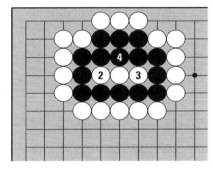

Diagram 7

Diagram 8:

White can play at 5, again at the center. Black is helpless to avoid capture.

Diagram 9:

Black has to play at the center first in order to live. With 1, Black has more than two eyes, so he can't be captured.

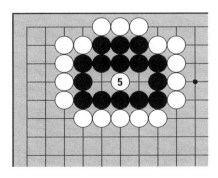

Diagram 8

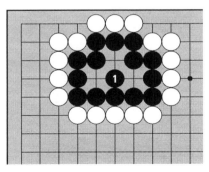

Diagram 9

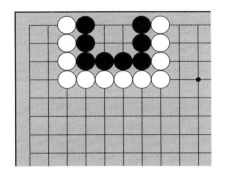

Diagram 10

Diagram 10:

Four points of territory in a square is a very bad shape in terms of life and death. This black group is dead without even being attacked.

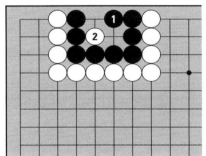

Diagram 11

Diagram 11:

Even if it is Black's turn, he can't live. If Black plays at 1, White can play 2 at the center.

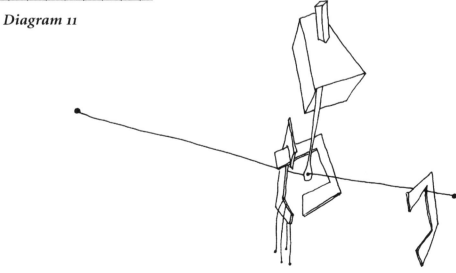

Even groups with five points of territory can be killed if they have a center point.

Diagram 12:

This group has five points arranged in a shape that to me looks like a Jeep. Even though Black has quite a few points, he has a soft spot at the center.

Diagram 13:

White 1 is the vital point. Black can't live.

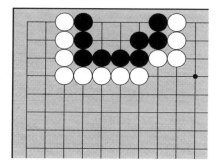

Diagram 12

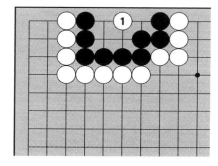

Diagram 13

Diagram 14:

If White wants to take these stones out, once again, White can just start filling in liberties at 2, 3, and 4. Both sides are now in atari, so Black can capture four stones at 5, but this is futile.

Diagram 15:

This is the result. Notice that Black now has the dead square shape. It's very useful to remember which shapes are alive and which are dead.

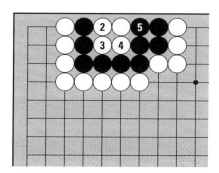

Diagram 14

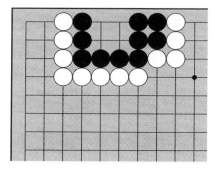

Diagram 15

3. LIFE AND DEATH SITUATIONS

Diagram 16:

Imagine this is your own game. What is the situation?

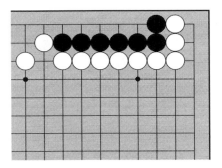

Diagram 16

Diagram 17:

If Black plays straight down at 1, Black makes four points of territory in a line. This is a living shape.

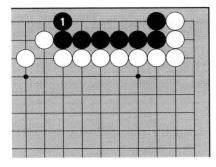

Diagram 17

Diagram 18:

If it's White's turn, White can play at 1. This reduces Black's potential space for making eyes. If Black blocks at 2, White can play at the center with 3. This is a dead shape.

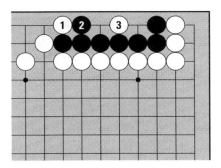

Diagram 18

Diagram 19:

Even though Black can capture White ◎ with 4, this only makes a false eye. How do you know it is false? Notice Black 4 is in atari if White blocks at 5.

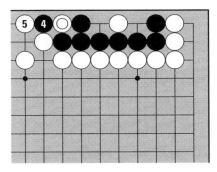

Diagram 19

Diagram 20:

What is the situation here?

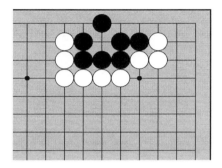

Diagram 20

Diagram 21:

Black has one eye, so he needs to make one more by playing straight down at 1. If it's White's turn, she can kill by playing at 1, preventing the second eye.

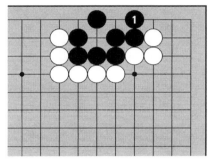

Diagram 21

Diagram 22:

Black 1 here is a mistake. Black can't make two eyes if White plays the throw-in at 2.

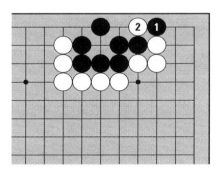

Diagram 22

Diagram 23:

Even though Black captures one stone at 3, Black is dead because White ◎ is a false eye.

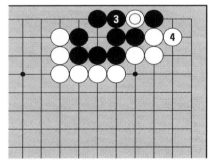

Diagram 23

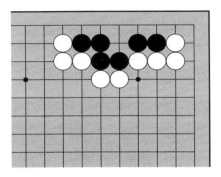

Diagram 24

Diagram 24:

Where does Black need to play to live?

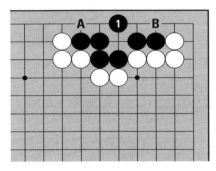

Diagram 25

Diagram 25:

In this shape, Black 1 is the vital point for life. Next Black can add the second eye by playing either A or B.

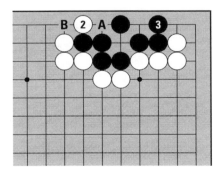

Diagram 26

Diagram 26:

If White plays at 2, Black plays 3. (Notice White can't make one eye false by playing at A, because Black could then capture two stones by playing at B.) If White plays 3 first, Black can play at 2.

Diagram 27:

White's turn to play. Try to kill Black.

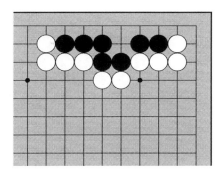

Diagram 27

Diagram 28:

If White plays at 1, Black can live by playing 2. Again, Black can make two eyes by playing either A or B.

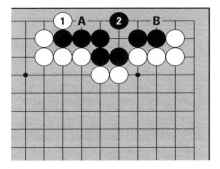

Diagram 28

Diagram 29:

White 1 is the vital point. Black can't live.

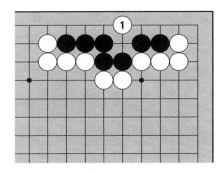

Diagram 29

Life and death is a very important part of playing Go. If you want to become strong, study life and death especially carefully.

TRY IT YOURSELF

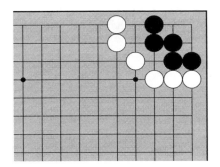

Problem 1

Problem 1:

Where does Black need a stone to live?

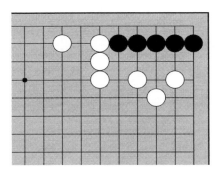

Problem 2

Problem 2:

If you were Black, where would you play to ensure life?

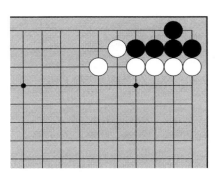

Problem 3

Problem 3:

How can White kill?

TRY IT YOURSELF

Problem 4:

White is not alive yet. Where does White need a stone?

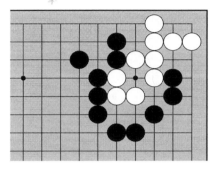

Problem 4

Problem 5:

White can kill. Where is the black group's vital point?

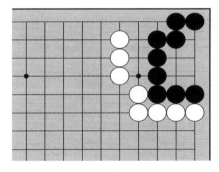

Problem 5

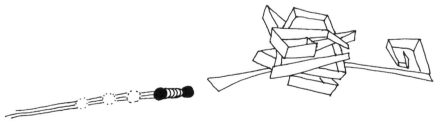

ANSWERS

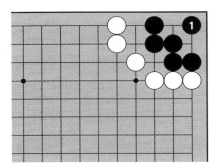

Answer 1

Answer 1:

Black makes two eyes with 1.

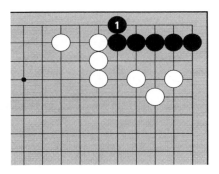

Answer 2a

Answer 2a:

You can make four points of territory in a line (a live shape) by coming straight down at 1.

Answer 2b

Answer 2b:

You also can live by playing 1 on the inside. If White plays the hane (the quick turn) at 2, you can make two eyes by blocking at 3. But compared to 2a, you have two points less territory.

ANSWERS

Answer 3:

White can kill with the hane at 1.

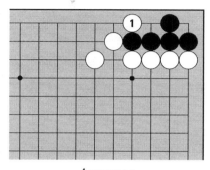

Answer 3

Answer 4:

White needs to play 1 in order to make the second eye. If Black plays 1, the second eye becomes false (notice three white stones would not be solidly connected to the main group). White would then die because her two points of territory in the corner are not separated.

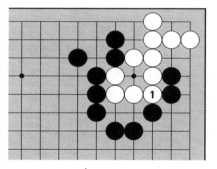

Answer 4

Answer 5:

If White plays 1 at the center, Black dies. Black has liberties on the outside, but can't escape or make two eyes.

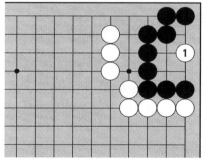

Answer 5

⑫

CAPTURING RACES

A capturing race is the most vicious kind of fight in Go. In a capturing race, you must block the liberties of your opponent's stones to capture them before they capture you.

1.   WHAT IS A CAPTURING RACE?

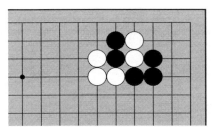

Diagram 1

Diagram 1:

Two black stones and two white stones are cutting each other off from their fellows. In this case, one side must capture the other.

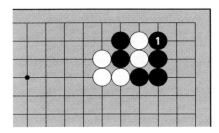

Diagram 2

Diagram 2:

If it's Black's turn to play, he quickly blocks a liberty at 1. Now White can be captured.

Diagram 3:

But if it is White's turn and she blocks a liberty at 1, now Black can be captured. This is a **capturing race** (also called a "liberty fight"). The goal is to capture enemy stones by quickly smothering them before they strangle you.

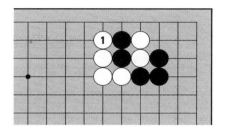

Diagram 3

Diagram 4:

Now three black stones and three white stones are cutting each other off. If it's White's turn to play, who will win the capturing race?

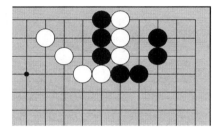

Diagram 4

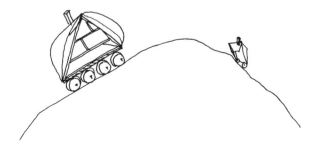

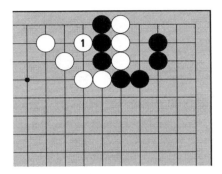

Diagram 5

Diagram 5:

Each side has three liberties. If White blocks a liberty first, she can capture.

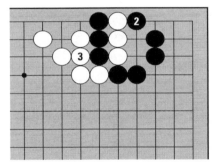

Diagram 6

Diagram 6:

Even if Black blocks a liberty at 2, White can play atari first at 3.

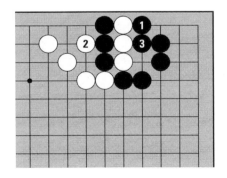

Diagram 7

Diagram 7:

If it had been Black's turn to play, he could have captured by blocking a liberty first. Whoever blocks the liberties first is the winner of this fight.

2. PREDICTING THE WINNER

To predict who will win a capturing race, count who has more liberties.

Diagram 8:

This is a capturing race between four black stones and four white stones. Both sides have three liberties. In this case, whoever blocks a liberty first will win.

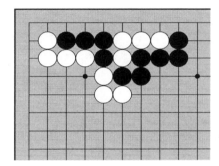

Diagram 8

Diagram 9:

If Black plays first, he can capture with 1 and 3.

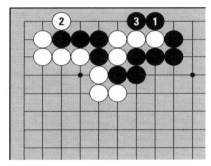

Diagram 9

Diagram 10:

Here the liberty at A isn't blocked, so the number of liberties is different. Black has four liberties and White has three.

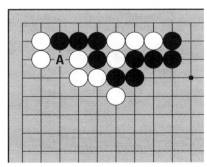

Diagram 10

Diagram 11:

In this case, even if White plays first, her four stones will be captured first if Black plays 2.

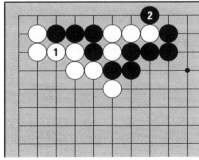

Diagram 11

3.   BLOCKING LIBERTIES

Outside liberties are one group's private liberty resource — they belong to one side only. **Inside liberties** are shared. In a capturing race, **block outside liberties first**.

Diagram 12:

Four black stones and five white stones are in a capturing race. Can you tell which liberties are outside and which are inside? Which liberties should Black block first?

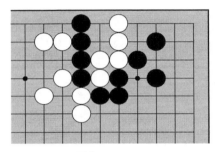

Diagram 12

Diagram 13:

Black has to block an outside liberty with 1. Next—

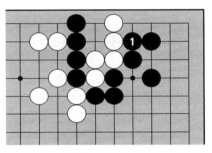

Diagram 13

Diagram 14:

Both sides continue blocking outside liberties with 2, 3, and 4. The result is dual life.

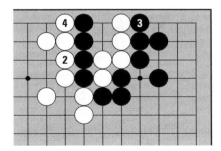

Diagram 14

Diagram 15:

If Black blocks an inside liberty with 1, he can be captured. Always block outside liberties first, since when you block inside liberties, you are blocking your own liberties as well as your opponent's.

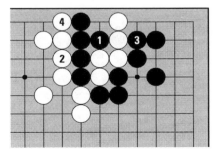

Diagram 15

TRY IT YOURSELF

Problem 1:

Which stones are cut off? Who will win the capturing race?

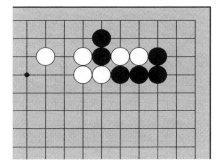

Problem 1

Problem 2:

Where can White play to capture three stones?

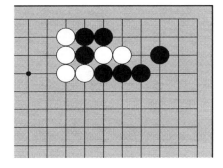

Problem 2

Problem 3:

In a capturing race, the motto is "Kill or be killed." How can Black kill?

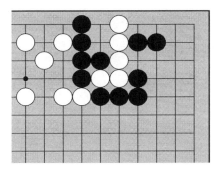

Problem 3

Problem 4:

The black and white groups have cut each other off. If it's Black's turn to play, what will happen?

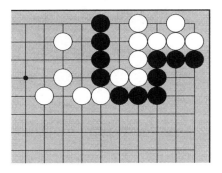

Problem 4

ANSWERS

Answer 1:

Black has two outside liberties and White has one, so even if it's White's turn, she can't win. If White blocks a liberty at 1, Black can play atari first with 2.

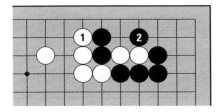

Answer 1

Answer 2:

White blocks at 1. She will win the resulting capturing race by one liberty.

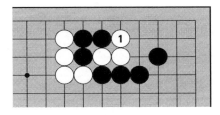

Answer 2

Answer 3:

Black blocks outside liberties first and wins by one liberty.

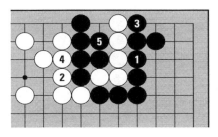

Answer 3a

If Black blocks liberties indiscriminately, White 2 and 4 put him in atari first.

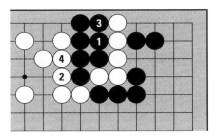

Answer 3b

Answer 4:

This position is not a capturing race. The white group that has been cut off has two eyes, so it is alive. You can't capture groups with two eyes.

THE HISTORY OF GO

Go is so ancient and widely revered that its origins are legendary. A popular story has it that the King of Yo (2356-2255 B.C.) asked his advisors for help with his belligerent and foolish son Danju. The Chief Minister delighted the court by inventing Go. "Now he will learn how to rule, by playing a game! Brilliant!" thought the King.

"It's boring," said Danju. "Whoever plays first wins." Danju didn't see that in Go, as in war, better strategy and tactics wins, regardless of who starts.

In disgust at his son's inability to appreciate Go, and in fear of what would happen if Danju were to command armies, the King appointed the Chief Minister heir to the kingdom.

What is almost certain is that Go developed several thousand years ago in or around what is now China. It probably had its origins in astronomy and divination, as can be evidenced in some terminology ("star point," for example) still in use today. It is believed that Go reached Korea some 2,000 years ago during the Three Kingdoms period in the first century B.C. However, a book of the time records that the Buddhist priest Dorim of Koguryo and King Gaero of Paekche played Go. This would indicate that Go spread from China to Korea even earlier.

It is thought that the Paekche Kingdom exported Go to Japan during the reign of Empress Suiko (500 A.D.). In Japan, Go was mainly an intellectual pastime of the royal court until it gained widespread popularity after Tokugawa, a master strategist and tactician, unified the nation around 1600 A.D.

Koreans used to begin play with setup stones on the corner star points until Cho Nam-chul brought the modern form of Go to Korea from Japan about fifty years ago. Modern Go, or Baduk as it is called in Korean, has spread across the whole country very quickly; it is now played by more than eight million people in Korea. By reading this book, you will learn an ancient "language" spoken by more than one hundred million people throughout the world. Slightly different customs apply in each country, but the basic rules and structure of the game are as old as the pyramids.

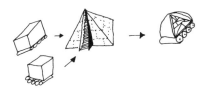

13

Ko Fighting

1. Ko Threats

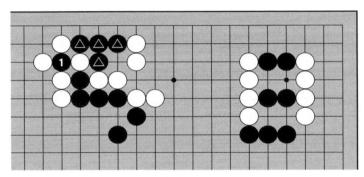

Diagram 1

Diagram 1:

If White connects at 1, the marked stones will be cut off with no eyes, so Black plays at 1, capturing a stone in ko. Black 1 is in atari, but according to the rule of ko, White may not capture a stone that has captured in ko immediately. She has to play somewhere else first.

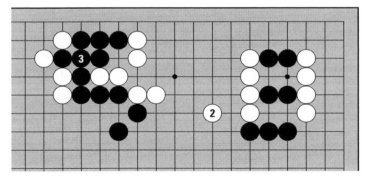

Diagram 2

Diagram 2:

If White plays 2, what will happen? Black doesn't need to answer 2, so he connects the ko at 3. White is a little disappointed about losing the chance to kill four stones. To fight the ko, White doesn't play at 2 —

Diagram 3:

When Black takes the ko at 1, White 2 here is a good idea. This move threatens to cut the bamboo joint, so if Black doesn't answer, White can cut off the two marked stones.

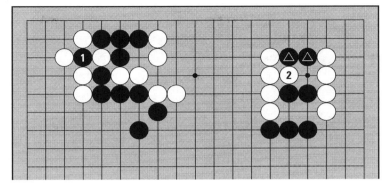

Diagram 3

Diagram 4:

Now if Black connects the ko at 3, White can carry out the threat with 4. White yielded the ko but cut off two stones as compensation, so she is satisfied.

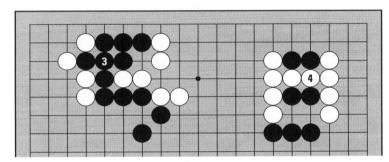

Diagram 4

Diagram 5:

When White plays at 1, suppose Black doesn't want to lose two stones. In that case he answers at 2. Then White can take back the ko at 3. White may capture here because she played somewhere else already with 1. White 1 is called a **ko threat**, a move that attempts to induce a response in order to take back a ko.

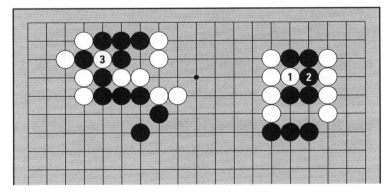

Diagram 5

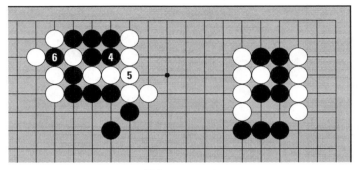

Diagram 6

Diagram 6:

This time it's Black's turn to play a ko threat. Black 4 puts the two cutting stones in atari, so White has to connect at 5. Now Black can take back the ko at 6.

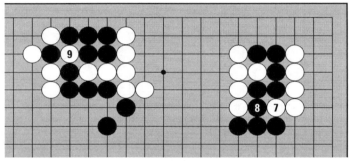

Diagram 7

Diagram 7:

White threatens to cut through a bamboo joint again with 7. Black connects at 8. Now White takes back the ko at 9. As you can see, ko fighting is about making ko threats and then taking back the ko. After White 9—

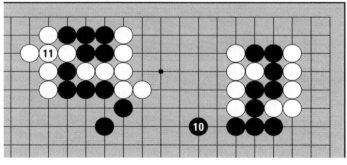

Diagram 8

Diagram 8:

What happens if Black plays 10? White doesn't have to answer, so she connects the ko at 11. White has won this ko. The five black stones at the top left are the spoils of this battle. The sequence of using ko threats and taking back the ko is called a **ko fight**.

Ko fighting is interesting but not easy to understand. The thing to come away with for now: if your opponent captures a stone in ko, use a ko threat and then you can either take back the ko or get something in exchange.

TRY IT YOURSELF

Problem 1:

Where can Black capture a stone in ko?

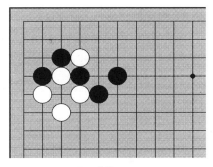

Problem 1

Problem 2:

After Black took the ko in the upper left corner at 1, White made a ko threat at 2. Should Black win the ko by capturing at A or answer the ko threat?

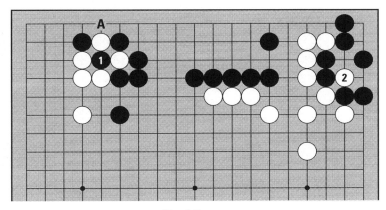

Problem 2

TRY IT YOURSELF

Problem 3:

White took the ko at 1 and Black made a ko threat at 2. White didn't answer the ko threat but connected at 3 (Black ▲). Now where should Black play?

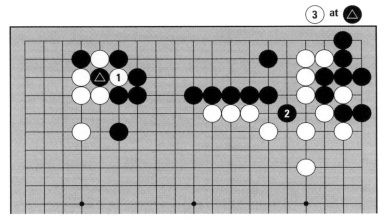

Problem 3

Problem 4:

When Black took the ko at 1, White played 2. Where should Black play?

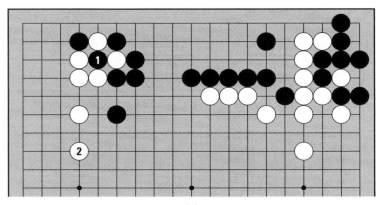

Problem 4

ANSWERS

Answer 1:

Black takes the ko at 1. If Black then wins the ko by capturing at A, he makes a lot of profit.

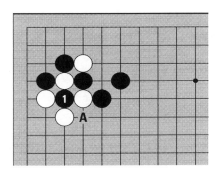

Answer 1

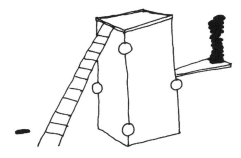

ANSWERS

Answer 2a:

If Black doesn't answer White 1 but elects to win the ko by capturing at 2 instead, White will capture two stones at 3. This is a bad time for Black to notice that the whole black group in the upper right has lost its eyes and is now dead. Even though Black won the ko, he has collapsed in the upper right.

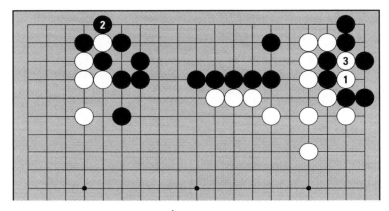

Answer 2a

Answer 2b:

Black should connect at 1. After White takes back the ko at 2, Black can make a ko threat and continue the ko fight.

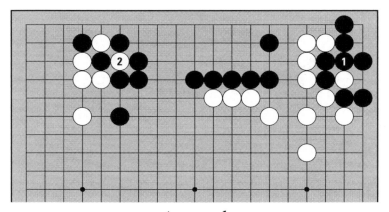

Answer 2b

ANSWERS

Answer 3:

Black △ *is a ko threat to cut off four stones if White doesn't answer, so naturally Black follows through by cutting at 1. The four stones can't escape and don't have any eyes, so they are dead.*

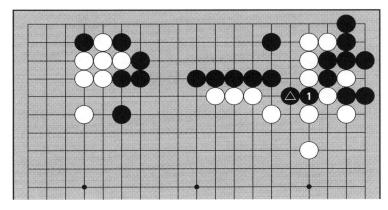

Answer 3

Answer 4:

Black doesn't need to answer White ◎ *, so Black ends the ko by capturing at 1. Black has won this ko.*

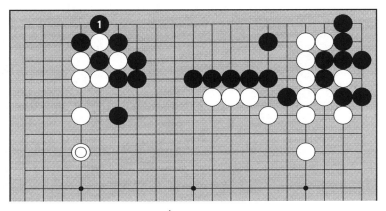

Answer 4

GO AND COMPUTERS

Computers and brains are totally different. In order to do anything, a computer must be given a precise list of very simple instructions. These instructions are executed by the machine one at a time in exactly the order specified, and each step has perfectly predictable results. In the brain, waves of activity pulse through our gray matter, alternately in electrical and chemical form, following myriad paths simultaneously, and interacting in complex, poorly understood ways. At the high level of thoughts and actions, we humans are scarcely aware of how our brains work. Our explanations of our own behavior often seem to be rationalization in hindsight rather than an accurate description of what went into our decision-making process.

Ever since computers were first built in the 1940s, people have debated whether these machines can be intelligent even in principle. This is a philosophical question, but an appealingly practical counterpoint was made by the grandfather of computing, Alan Turing, in 1950: If a computer were indistinguishable from a human in an extended conversation, the question of whether it were intelligent would become purely an academic one of definition. Simply put, if machines act intelligently enough, then for all practical purposes, they are intelligent.

The field of computer science concerned with making computers behave intelligently is called Artificial Intelligence. One of the first tasks undertaken in that field was to make a computer play chess. As Claude Shannon put it in his seminal article of 1950, "chess is generally considered to require thinking for skillful play; a solution of this problem will force us either to admit the possibility of mechanized thinking, or to further restrict our concept of 'thinking.'"

Since then, chess programs have been developed to a remarkable level. In 1994, Garry Kasparov, World Chess Champion, lost to a computer for the first time, and the time when chess computers will be stronger than the best human players is within sight. Unfortunately, chess programs do not seem very intelligent in the way they work. Chess computers operate by performing exhaustive searches through many millions of future possibilities to choose their moves. The strongest computers examine on the order of a million positions each second. Clearly, this is nothing like the way humans play.

GO AND COMPUTERS

This "brute force" approach is not applicable to Go. For one thing, brute force depends absolutely on the ability to perform a quick, accurate positional analysis, but it is qualitatively more difficult to evaluate a Go position than a chess position. In particular, in Go deep analysis is often required just to decide which stones on the board are alive and which are dead. A single mistake in this analysis could easily throw off a computer's evaluation by 100 points. Even if quick, accurate analysis were possible, the relatively large size of the Go board means that billions of times more future positions would have to be searched through each turn to reach the same level of accuracy that chess computers now have.

Because the brute force approach to Go is closed for the foreseeable future, Go is a much more interesting computing problem than chess. Go programmers must try to replace exhaustive search with expert knowledge as human players do; they must approximate human perception, judgment, and reasoning. So far, there has been scant success. As things stand now, the best Go computers play only at the level of an experienced beginner. If you've read this book, you are already around the level of the most sophisticated computer. The challenging field of Go computing remains wide open.

David Mechner

August 1994

David Mechner studied Go at the academy of the Japan Go Association, and neuroscience at New York University, and has worked extensively on the problem of computer Go. As predicted, Kasparov lost to IBM's Deep Blue in a highly-publicized match in 1997, and as of 2010, computer Go-playing programs remain at the lower levels.

ENDING AND COUNTING

1. WHEN THE GAME IS OVER

Black and White take turns, each playing one stone until the game is over. Since the aim of Go is to surround territory, we often say the game is over when no more territory can be made or lost. At that point, the players each pass and then fill in the neutral points. In some rule sets, the game isn't officially over until all the neutral points are filled. You can always fill in a neutral point if you aren't sure if the game is over.

Diagram 1:

This is the last stage of a game on a 13 x 13 board. There are some unfinished areas. Where are they?

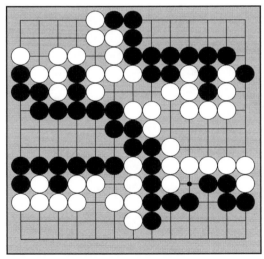

Diagram 1

Diagram 2:

The walls of territory are not yet complete at A and B. So if it is White's turn—

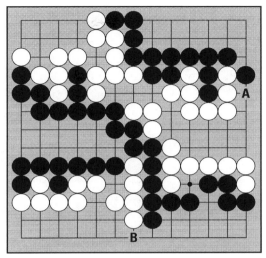

Diagram 2

Diagram 3:

White blocks at 1. Black connects at 2 and this area is finished. Next White plays the hane at 3. Black blocks at 4 and White connects at 5. Now this area is finished. Only the neutral points marked X are left. No more territory can be made or lost, so the players confirm that the game is over.

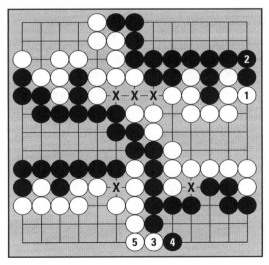

Diagram 3

2. FILLING IN NEUTRAL POINTS

The neutral points aren't territory, so it doesn't affect the score if one side fills in more with regular counting and scoring. In practice, many players take turns filling them in, since it could fill in a liberty that would require a connection, or you could be using a rule set where players take turns playing the neutral points before the game is officially over.

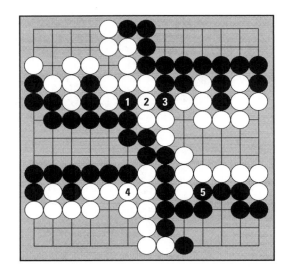

Diagram 4:

The neutral points are filled in the sequence from 1 to 5. Filling in neutral points does not profit either side. But when they are filled, there are matters that demand special attention.

Diagram 4

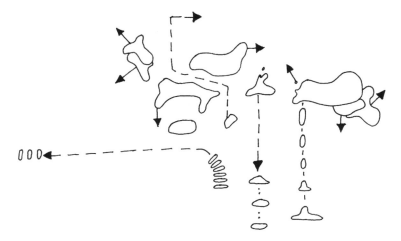

Diagram 5:

Only the neutral points at A and B remain. Take care when filling them, as when liberties are blocked, weak points are revealed.

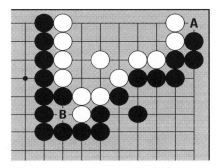

Diagram 5

Diagram 6:

Black fills a neutral point at 1, which also takes away one of White's liberties. If White fills in the other neutral point with 2 —

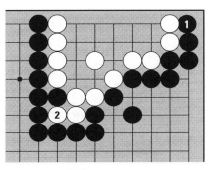

Diagram 6

Diagram 7:

Black can cut at 3. The two white stones will be captured and part of White's territory will be destroyed.

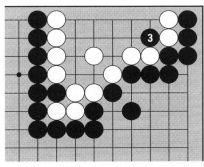

Diagram 7

Diagram 8:

When Black fills the neutral point at 1, White has to connect at 2 to prevent a breakthrough.

Neutral points have no value, but filling them in can be dangerous. Be careful: there's still a bit of reading to do even after the territorial borders are complete.

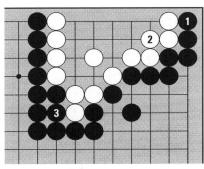

Diagram 8

3. DISPOSITION OF DEAD STONES

After all the neutral points are filled, players take out each other's dead stones.

Diagram 9:

Let's look at this completed game on a 9 x 9 board. Black and White each have dead stones in their territories. These stones have to be taken out.

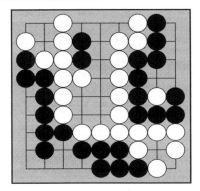

Diagram 9

Diagram 10:

At the end of the game, you don't need to play at the places marked with an A to capture; dead stones are just removed.

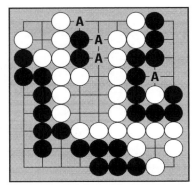

Diagram 10

Diagram 11:

The players have taken out each other's dead stones from the places marked X.

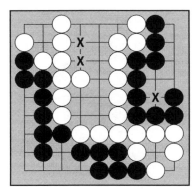

Diagram 11

Diagram 12:

The players put the dead stones (White ◎ and Black ▲) in their opponent's territory. Each dead stone reduces territory by one point. If you have captured or killed ten stones, you can reduce your opponent's territory by ten points.

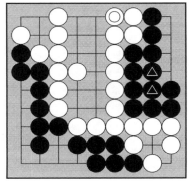

Diagram 12

4. ARRANGING TERRITORIES

After the neutral points are filled and dead stones used to reduce territory, arrange and count the territory left.

Diagram 13:

All the neutral points have been filled, and captured or dead stones used to reduce territory. We are now in the counting phase.

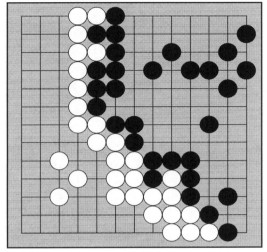

Diagram 13

Diagram 14:

For easy counting, arrange the stones to form rectangular shapes without destroying the territorial borderlines. Black has 57 points and White has 52 points, so Black wins by 5 points.

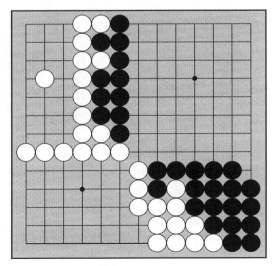

Diagram 14

TRY IT YOURSELF

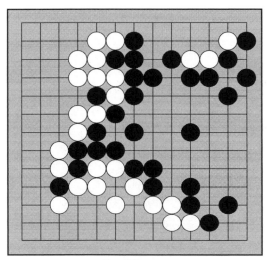

Problem 1

Problem 1:

This is a game on a 13 x 13 board. The game is almost over but there are still some places that are unfinished. Where are they?

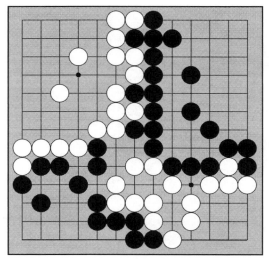

Problem 2

Problem 2:

This game is over, with only neutral points remaining. Where are they?

TRY IT YOURSELF

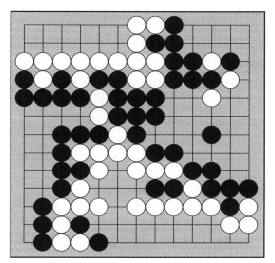

Problem 3

Problem 3:

After this game ended, the players filled in all the neutral points. Now they must fill in each other's territories with the dead stones. Where are they?

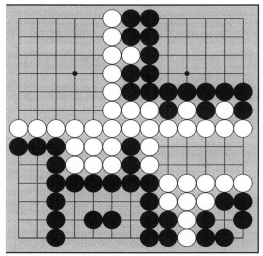

Problem 4

Problem 4:

The players then arranged the territories to make rectangles. How much territory does each side have? Who is the winner and by how many points?

ANSWERS

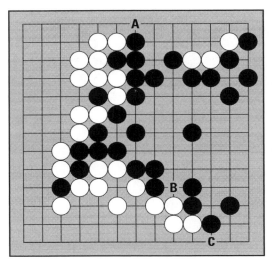

Answer 1a

Answer 1a:

The incomplete areas are at A, B, and C. When the borders in these areas are finished, the game is over.

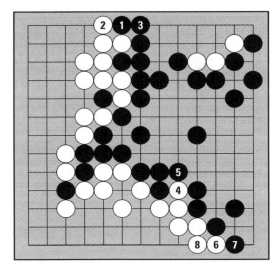

Answer 1b

Answer 1b:

The ending sequence is shown from Black 1 to White 8. The moves made to complete the territorial borderlines are called the endgame.

ANSWERS

Answer 2a:

There are six neutral points marked X. Notice—

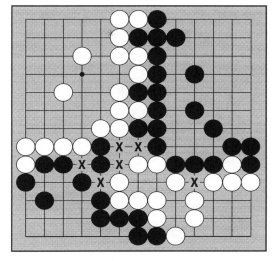

Answer 2a

Answer 2b:

When White fills the neutral point at 1, Black has to connect at 2. (White 1 threatens the diagonal connection between the two black stones and the corner group.) The remaining neutral points are then filled. It doesn't matter which ones you fill, as long as you watch your weak points.

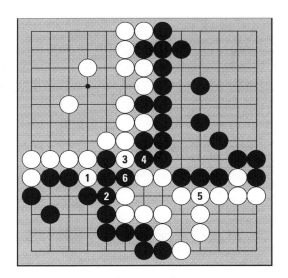

Answer 2b

ANSWERS

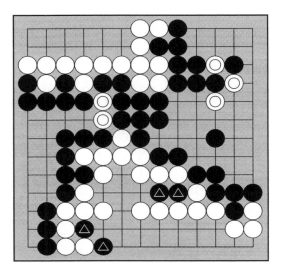

Answer 3

Answer 3:

The four marked black stones and the five marked white stones are dead. These stones are just taken out, and put in their color's territory.

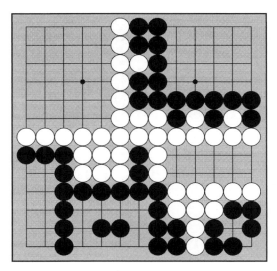

Answer 4

Answer 4:

Black has 42 points and White has 40 points, so Black wins by 2 points.

SAMPLE OPENINGS

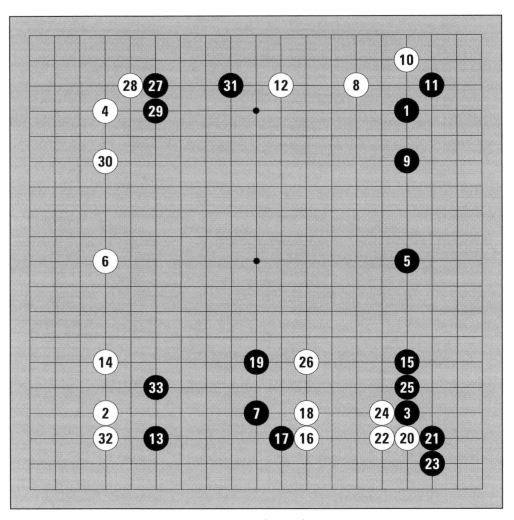

Game 1 (1 – 33)

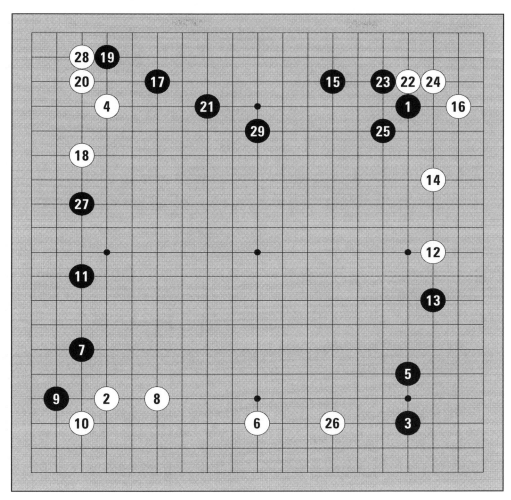

Game 2 (1 – 29)

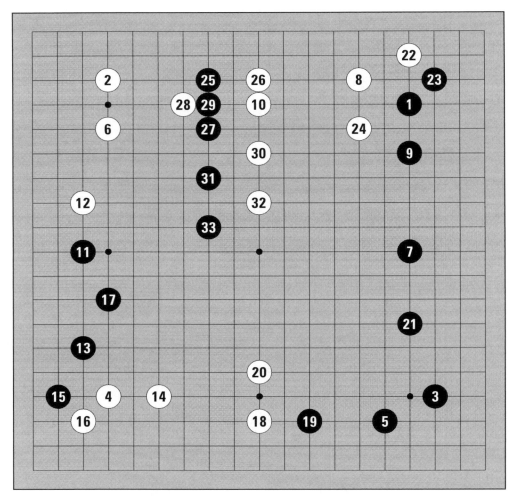

Game 3 (1 – 33)

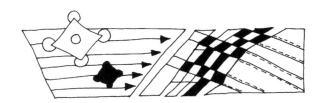

Index

Note on names: Chinese, Japanese, and Korean names in this book are given family name first. Jeong Soo-hyun's family name is Jeong.

Read the entire series!

Learn to Play Go

SAMARKAND
Play Smart!

About the Authors

Janice Kim was born in Illinois in 1969. She became the first female student at the Korean Go Academy in 1983 and entered the professional dan ranks in Korea in 1987, the first Westerner ever to do so. She won the Fuji Women's Championship in 1984, took second place in the World Youth Championship in 1985, and third place in the EBS Cup in 1994. She was promoted to 3 dan in 2003.

After graduating from New York University, Ms. Kim authored the five books of the Learn to Play Go series and founded the online Go company Samarkand. In 2008, in an effort to explore similarities in strategy games, she played in the World Poker Tour's Women's Championship in Las Vegas and placed fourth. She currently resides in the San Francisco bay area with her husband and two children.

Timothy Greenfield-Sanders

Jeong Soo-hyun was born in Korea in 1956. Since entering the professional dan ranks in 1973, he has played in numerous championship leagues, winning the Shin Wang title in 1986. He was promoted to 8 dan in 1994, and 9 dan in 1997.

A well-known teacher, Mr. Jeong has written more than twenty books and is a popular commentator on Korean television. He served a term as President of the Korean Professional Go Association, the youngest person ever to hold this prestigious post. Now a university professor teaching Go, he lives in Seoul with his wife and two children.

Hankook Kiwon

33305680R00104